Andrew J Cleaveland

The School Harmonist

Comprising Psalm and hymn tunes in general use

Andrew J Cleaveland

The School Harmonist
Comprising Psalm and hymn tunes in general use

ISBN/EAN: 9783337298579

Printed in Europe, USA, Canada, Australia, Japan

Cover: Foto ©Thomas Meinert / pixelio.de

More available books at **www.hansebooks.com**

THE
SCHOOL HARMONIST:

COMPRISING

Psalm and Hymn Tunes in General Use;

TOGETHER WITH

SEVERAL TUNES AND CHANTS,

DESIGNED AS AN ACCOMPANIMENT TO

THE MANUAL OF DEVOTION FOR SCHOOLS,

(BY N. C. BROOKS, A. M.,)

AND FOR THE USE OF

Choirs, Singing Schools, and Private Families.

By ANDREW J. CLEAVELAND,
PROFESSOR OF MUSIC IN THE BALTIMORE FEMALE COLLEGE.

NEW YORK:
PUBLISHED BY A. S. BARNES & BURR,
51 & 53 JOHN STREET.
SOLD BY BOOKSELLERS, GENERALLY, THROUGHOUT THE UNITED STATES.
1860.

PREFACE.

Regarding it as of the utmost importance to the prosperity and happiness of our country, that the minds of the young should early be imbued with moral and religious sentiments, I have long been convinced that in all our systems of education, religious instruction should form a part of the daily exercises in school.

In accordance with these views, and to supply more immediately a want felt in our own institution, I prepared, some time since, the MANUAL OF DEVOTION FOR SCHOOLS, comprising a series of religious exercises without any sectarian bias, which present the great truths of Christianity in a way calculated to interest the youthful mind in the study of the Bible, and to impress the heart with feelings of a religious and devotional character.

These exercises consist in part of readings and responses by the teachers and scholars, and as they are made up of extracts from the Bible, they are entirely unexceptionable to any denomination of Christians.

The Chorister and School Harmonist, is designed as an accompaniment to the Manual of Devotion. It contains the elements of musical science, presented to the mind of the scholar in a series of easy lessons, and the hymns of the Manual set to appropriate tunes, with many other hymns and chants,—the whole arranged with care by a distinguished musical professor, and forming a neat and elegant collection of religious music, suited for choirs, schools, and private families. We commend it with confidence to the patronage of the public.

N. C. BROOKS.

BALTIMORE FEMALE COLLEGE,

EDITOR'S PREFACE.

In presenting the Chorister and School Harmonist to the public, we beg leave to state that the contents have been selected and newly harmonized with much care, or have been composed expressly for the work. We trust it will be found an acceptable addition to the number of music books already in use.

To make the book of a portable size, we have put two parts on a staff, with the whole hymn interlined in a manner convenient for singing. The names of the hymns are made to conform to those previously published in the "Manual of Devotion," and hence the change in some old favorites.

Should the organist sometimes find the notes of the tunes beyond the reach of his hands, he is at liberty to play the base an octave higher. If the organ has a pedal, it will of course obviate the difficulty. This trifling inconvenience to the accompanyist, caused by a more free carrying out of the melody of each voice, will, we hope, be more than compensated by the beauties added to the music.

METRICAL INDEX.

L. M.
Alfreton,	65
All Saints,	42
Arnold,	38
Battee,	58
Brooklyn,	70
Cleaveland,	39
Clinton,	55
Companion	72
Dresden,	62
Dudley,	61
Duke Street,	73
El Paran,	50
Gratitude,	45
Hamburg,	71
Hamner,	46
Hebron,	47
Hingham,	56
Humility,	76
Jura,	77
Lightner,	172
Malan,	59
Mendon,	41
Munich,	43
New Sabbath,	40
Old Hundred,	69
Prince,	75
Raymond,	44
Rockingham,	57
Sabaoth,	48
Sargent,	06
Saxton,	60
South Street,	51
Stonefield,	78
Temple Street,	52
Thorpe,	74
Valentia,	49
Ware,	64
Warefield,	68
Welton,	233
Windham,	53
Wisdom,	54

C. M.
Albert,	104
Arlington,	97
Balerma,	113
Bethlehem,	88
Bolton,	126
Brattle Street,	100
Collister,	110
Conway,	92
Covington,	120
Dedham,	102
Delight,	96
Devizes,	93
Devon,	79
Doddridge,	98
Downs,	127
Dwight,	96
Egremont,	122
Ephesus,	106
Fear,	111
Florence,	85
Fountain,	116
Franklin,	81
Germany,	123
Gillett,	117
Hammond,	109
Hanover,	90
Happiness,	86
Heber,	80
Heiner,	134
Howard,	84
Iddo,	105
Irish,	130
Jerusalem,	114
Jewell,	108
Lanesboro,	89
Litchfield,	129
Marlow,	128
Naomi,	131
Ortonville,	91
Perpetuity,	119
Piety,	82
Pilgrim,	107
Shepham,	94
Shepherd,	87
Stoneville,	99
Tallis,	124
Unity,	103
Varina,	132
Warwick,	118
Waugh,	112
Woodland,	95
Zerah,	125

S. M.
Alva,	137
Backus,	143
Ballston,	142
Cranbrook,	136

METRICAL INDEX.

Desire, ...153
Doomsday, ...145
Dover, ...156
Flint, ...157
Hart, ...140
Henshaw, ...158
Hoffman, ...152
Laban, ...101
Lane, ...160
Lansdale, ...138
Lathrop, ...141
Lisbon, ...155
Marcus, ...144
Morris, ...163
Murdoch, ...146
Painsville, ...150
Palermo, ...154
Silver Street, ...135
Slicer, ...162
St. Thomas, ...148
Teleman, ...149
Thatcher, ...147
Watchman, ...159

H. M.
Lenox, ...164
Plummer, ...174
Solitude, ...176

P. M.
Happy Land, ...183
Washburn, ...219

L. P. M.
Ashton, ...166
Nashville, ...168
Newcourt, ...170

C. P. M.
Arnon, ...178
Brightness, ...202

7s.
Acton, ...198
Betah, ...206
Christian Pilgrim, ...220
Heath, ...186
Hotham, ...168
Otto, ...185
Pilgrim, ...201
Rock of Ages, ...189
Snowfield...............184
Spring, ...190
Stockton, ...218
Wilmot, ...191

8s and 7s.
Little, ...173
Mozart, ...180
Smyrna, ...182
Sabbath School Hymn, ...200

8s, 7s and 4s.
Haydn, ...204
Orford, ...199

12s and 11s.
Gibbons, ...228

7s and 6s.
Chaney, ...192

6s and 4s.
America, ...217

6s.
Sabbath, ...194

ANTHEMS, SENTENCES, CHANTS, &c.

Come unto me, all ye that labor, ...230
Gloria Patria, No. 1.—" Glory be to the Father," 210
Gloria Patria, No. 2.—" Glory be to the Father," 212
Holy, holy, holy, Lord, God Almighty, ...236
How amiable are thy tabernacles, ...237
How lovely is Zion, ...222
Lord, thou hast been our dwelling place, ...238
The Beatitudes—" *Blessed are the poor in spirit,*" 235
The last beam is shining, ...214
The Lord himself, the mighty Lord, ...196
The Lord is in his holy temple, ...207
The Lord is my Shepherd, ...234
The Lord will comfort Zion, ...225

ELEMENTS OF MUSIC.

LESSON FIRST.

THE STAFF.

1. The staff consists of five horizontal, parallel lines, with the four intermediate spaces.

2. It is used to regulate and determine the pitch of musical sounds, and is written thus:

```
Fourth Space. ─────────────────  5th line.
Third Space.  ─────────────────  4th line.
Second Space. ─────────────────  3d line.
First Space.  ─────────────────  2d line.
              ─────────────────  1st line.
```

3. In counting the degrees of the staff, we always commence at the bottom and count up, as above.

4. Each line, and each space of the staff is called a Degree.

5. There are nine degrees on the staff, five lines, and four spaces.

6. We sometimes wish to represent higher sounds than can be represented on the staff, in which case we use added lines above; thus:

```
Fourth Space above. ─────────  3d added line above.
Third Space above.  ─────────  2d added line above.
Second Space above. ─────────  1st added line above.
First Space above.  ─────────
                    ─────────
                    ─────────
                    ─────────
                    ─────────
```

And, put the notes on them, or on the space thus added.

7. We sometimes wish to represent lower sounds than can be represented on the staff, in which case we use added lines below; thus:

```
                    ─────────
                    ─────────
                    ─────────
                    ─────────
First Space below.  ─────────  1st added line below.
Second Space below. ─────────  2d added line below.
Third Space below.  ─────────  3d added line below.
Fourth Space below.
```

8. In counting the added degrees, we always commence nearest the staff.

QUESTIONS.

1. Of what does the Staff consist?
2. For what is it used?
3. How do we count the degrees of the Staff?
4. What is called a degree?
5. How many degrees on the Staff?
6. If we wish to represent higher sounds than can be represented on the Staff, what must we do?
7. If we wish to represent lower sounds than can be represented on the staff, what must we do?
8. How do we count the added degrees?

LESSON SECOND.

NOTES.

1. Musical characters of different forms called notes, are used to represent, and regulate, sounds of different length, in regard to duration of time.

2. We use eight different kinds of notes.

3.

NAME.	FORM.
Double note.	Open head and two lines each side.
Whole note.	Open head.
Half note.	Open head and line.
Quarter note.	Closed head and line.
Eighth note.	Line and hook.
Sixteenth note.	Two hooks.
Thirty-second note.	Three hooks.
Sixty-fourth note.	Four hooks.

4. The double note, and Sixty-fourth note, are seldom used.

QUESTIONS.

1. Those characters used to represent sounds are called what?
2. How many kinds of notes are used?
3. Name them? Their Form?
4. Which notes are seldom used?

LESSON THIRD.

RESTS.

1. Rests are used to indicate silence.
2. Each note has its corresponding rest, except the double *note*.
3. The rests receive their names from their corresponding notes.
4. There are seven rests, as follows, thus:

5. NAME.   FORM.
Whole rest.   Block under a line.
Half rest.   Block over a line.
Quarter rest.   Perpendicular line, and hook to the right.
Eighth rest.   Perpendicular line and hook to the left.
Sixteenth rest.   Two hooks.
Thirty-second rest.   Three hooks.
Sixty-fourth rest.   Four hooks.

QUESTIONS.

1. What are those characters called which indicate silence?
2. Which note does not have a corresponding rest?
3. How do the rests receive their names?
4. How many rests are used in music?
5. Name them? Their form?

LESSON FOURTH.

CLEFS.

1. The first seven letters of the Alphabet, viz, A, B, C, D, E, F, and G, are used to designate the lines, and spaces of the staff.

2. We have two characters, called the G clef, and the F clef, which are used to designate how the letters are placed on the staff.

3. The G Clef is formed thus:

And shows that G, is on the second line.

4. Letters on the staff with the G Clef.

5. The F clef is formed thus:

And shows that F is on the fourth line.

6. Letters on the staff with the F clef.

ELEMENTS OF MUSIC.   5

QUESTIONS.

1. How many letters of the Alphabet are used in music?
2. What characters are used to show how the letters are placed on the staff?
3. What is the G clef used for?
4. Name the letters on the staff with the G clef.
5. What is the F clef used for?
6. Name the letters on the staff with the F clef.

LESSON FIFTH.

THE SCALE.

1. The scale consists of eight consecutive notes, written one above another, thus:

SCALE OF C MAJOR, NATURAL POSITION. G CLEF.

Numerals.	1	2	3	4	5	6	7	8
Names.	Do	Re	Mi	Fa	Sol	La	Si	Do
Letters.	C	D	E	F	G	A	B	C

2. SCALE OF C MAJOR, NATURAL POSITION. F CLEF

	1	2	3	4	5	6	7	8
	Do	Re	Mi	Fa	Sol	La	Si	Do
	C	D	E	F	G	A	B	C

3. The difference of pitch between any two notes of the scale is called an interval.

4. The interval between any note and the next note above, or below, is called the interval of a second.

[1*]

5. We have two kinds of seconds in the scale, Major (or large,) and Minor (or small,) and in the minor scale we have the augmented second.

6. The intervals between three and four, and between seven and eight, are minor seconds, and all the rest are major seconds.

7. We have two kinds of scales, from which music is composed; the major as above, and its relative minor, and we have also the chromatic scale.

8. They differ only in the order of intervals, which difference changes the character of the music. The minor being of a more solemn and mournful nature, and consequently better adapted to funeral and other solemn occasions.

QUESTIONS.

1. Of what does the scale consist?

2. Where is one (or Do,) in the natural scale, G clef! Where in the F clef?

3. What is the difference of pitch between any two notes called?

4. What is the difference of pitch between any note and the next above or below called?

5. How many kinds of seconds are used in the scale? What are they called?

6. Where are the minor seconds found in the major scale?

7. How many kinds of scales are in use? What are they called?

8. In what do they differ? What effect does this difference produce? What is the difference between the character of Major and Minor music?

LESSON SIXTH.

TIME.

1. During the performance of a piece of music a certain portion of time must necessarily pass away.

2. We divide music into small portions called measures, by using a character called a bar.

3. A bar is a perpendicular line. When used in music it is drawn across the staff, thus:

4. A measure is the space between two bars, as above.

ELEMENTS OF MUSIC.

5. There are four kinds of time.

6. They are called, Double, Triple, Quadruple, and Sextuple.

7. Double time has two beats in a measure, *down* and *up*, accented on the first part of each measure, and counted *one, two*.

8. Triple time has three beats, *down, left,* and *up;* accented on the first part of each measure, and counted *one, two, three.*

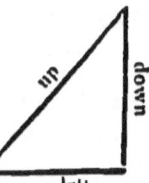

9. Quadruple time has four beats, *down, left, right,* and *up,* accented on the first, and third parts of each measure, and counted *one, two, three, four.*

10. Sextuple time has six beats, *two down, left, right,* and *two up,* accented on the first and fourth part of each measure, and counted *one, two, three, four, five, six.*

NOTE. In quick movements sextuple time is frequently beat as double time, giving one beat to each accented part of the measure.

QUESTIONS.

1. What part of music do we learn by Lesson Sixth?
2. How is music divided into measures?
3. What is a bar?
4. What is a measure?
5. How many kinds of time are used in music?
6. What are they called?
7. How many beats has double time? How are they made? How is it accented?
8. Triple time has how many beats? How is it accented? How are the beats made?
9. Quadruple time has how many beats? How are they made? How is it accented?
10. Sextuple time has how many beats? How are they made? How is it accented?

LESSON SEVENTH.

TIME, CONTINUED.

1. Figures are used in fractional form at the commencement of every piece of music, to signify the kind of time.
2. The upper figure numerates the parts in each measure.
3. The lower figure denominates the kind of note used on each part of a measure.
4. Each measure must receive the value of what the figures call for, either in notes or rests.
5. In double time the upper figure is always 2, as the following examples will illustrate.

6. In triple time the upper figure is always 3, as follows:

7. In quadruple time the upper figure is always 4.

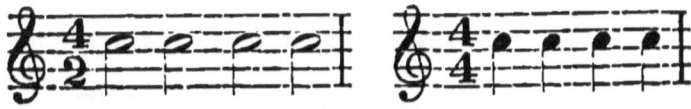

8. In Sextuple time the upper figure is always 6.

QUESTIONS.

1. What are used at the commencement of a piece of music to designate the kind of time?
2. What do we understand by the upper figure?
3. What do we understand by the lower figure?
4. What must each measure receive?
5. What is always the upper figure in double time?
6. What is always the upper figure in triple time?
7. In quadruple time what is the upper figure?
8. In sextuple time what is the upper figure?

NOTE. The teacher will here illustrate on the black board all the varieties of time, both in primitive and derived forms of measure.

LESSON EIGHTH.

OTHER MUSICAL CHARACTERS EXPLAINED.

1. Triplet. A figure three placed over or under any three notes, directs that the notes be sung or played in the time of two of the same kind.

2. Tie, or Slur. A tie, or slur connects such notes as are to be sung to one syllable. It is also sometimes used to designate the legato style.

3. Staccato marks. Staccato marks placed over or under notes show that they are to be performed in a short, distinct, and disconnected manner.

4. Dots of addition. A dot placed after a note, adds one half to its length.

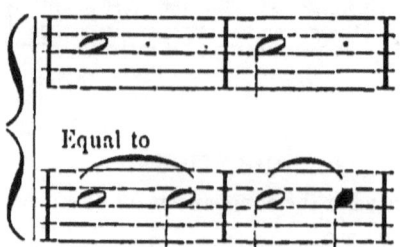

5. If there are two dots, the last one adds one half the value of the first one.

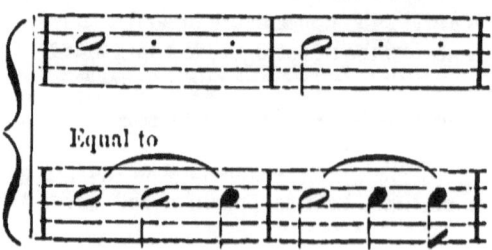

ELEMENTS OF MUSIC.   11

6. **Pause, or Hold.** A pause, or hold placed over or under a note denotes that the sound is to be sustained longer than its usual time.

7. **Crescendo.** A crescendo denotes a gradual increase of volume or power of sound.

8. **Diminuendo.** A diminuendo denotes a gradual decrease of volume, or power of sound.

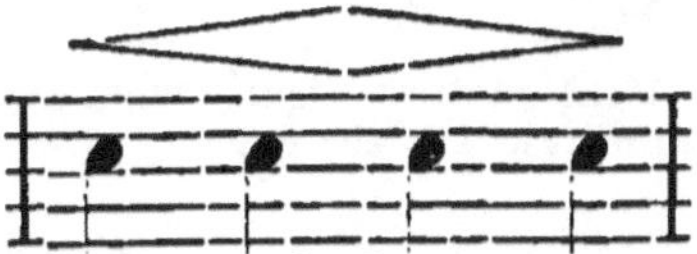

9. **Swell.** A swell combines the characters of the crescendo, and diminuendo, denoting a gradual increase and then a gradual decrease of volume or power of sound.

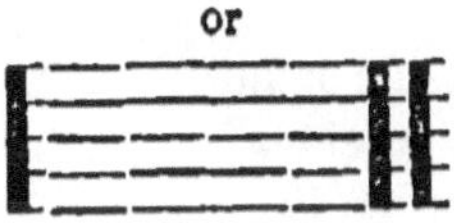

10. **Double Bar.** Double Bar shows the end of phrase, or the end A double bar usually a strain, or musical of a line in poetry.

11. **A Close.** A close shows the end of a tune, or musical composition.

12. **Repeat.** A repeat shows that a certain portion of a piece of music is to be sung or played over again.

 Del Segno.

13. **Sharp.** A sharp placed before a note directs the pitch of the note to be raised a minor second.

14. **Flat.** A flat placed before a note directs the pitch of the note to be lowered a minor second.

15. **Natural.** A natural placed before a note previously flatted or sharped, restores it to its original sound.

16. **Signatures.** Flats or sharps placed at the beginning of a piece of music, are called Signatures.

17. Signatures signify what key the music is in, or what letter is taken as 1 of the scale.

QUESTIONS.

1. What is a triplet?
2. What is the use of the tie or slur?
3. What do staccato marks show?
4. What is the use of the dot?
5. If there are two dots what is the use of the second one?
6. What is the use of the pause or hold?
7. What does a crescendo denote?
8. A diminuendo?
9. A swell?
10. What does the double bar show us?
11. What do we understand by the close?
12. What is the use of the repeat?
13. What is the use of the sharp?
14. What is the use of the flat?
15. What is the use of the natural?
16. Flats or sharps placed at the beginning of a piece of music are called what?
17. What do we understand by signatures?

LESSON NINTH.

TRANSPOSITION OF THE SCALE.

1. The scale is transposed, when it is not in its natural position.

2. It is in its natural position when the letter C is 1, or when 1 is written on that letter.

3. When a piece of music is composed from the scale in its natural position, we see no sharps, or flats at the commencement, and the signature is said to be natural.

4. Flats and sharps are used to preserve the regular order of intervals in the scale, when transposed.

5. The regular order of intervals are, from one to two, a major second, from two to three, a major second, from three to four, a minor second, from four to five, five to six, and six to seven, all major seconds, and from seven to eight, a minor second.

6. The minor seconds occur between the letters, E and F, and B and C, in the natural scale.

NOTE. See scale in Lesson Fifth.

The following eight scales are all the transpositions in common use, and if the pupil thoroughly understands them, all the rest will be easily learned.

7. Signature of one sharp.   Key of G.

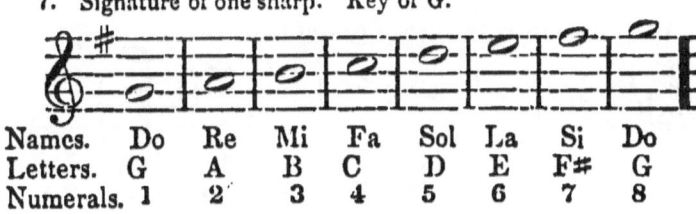

Names.	Do	Re	Mi	Fa	Sol	La	Si	Do
Letters.	G	A	B	C	D	E	F#	G
Numerals.	1	2	3	4	5	6	7	8

8. Signature of two sharps.   Key of D

	Do	Re	Mi	Fa	Sol	La	Si	Do
	D	E	F#	G	A	B	C#	D
	1	2	3	4	5	6	7	8

[2]

ELEMENTS OF MUSIC.

9. Signature of three sharps. Key of A.

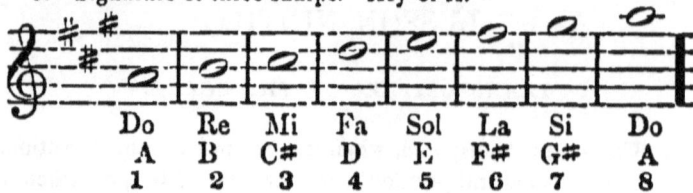

10. Signature of four sharps. Key of E.

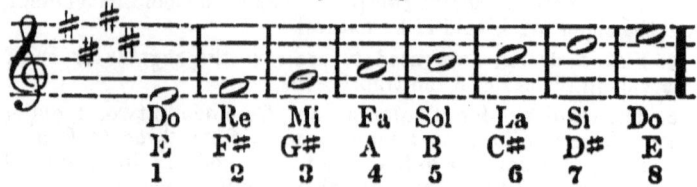

11. Signature of one flat. Key of F.

12. Signature of two flats. Key of Bb.

13. Signature of three flats. Key of Eb.

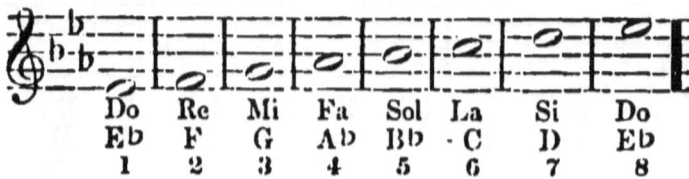

ELEMENTS OF MUSIC.

14. Signature of four flats. Key of A♭.

The following eight scales with the F clef, are intended for those wishing to learn Bass and Tenor.

15. Signature of one sharp. Key of G. F Clef.

16. Signature of two sharps. Key of D. F Clef.

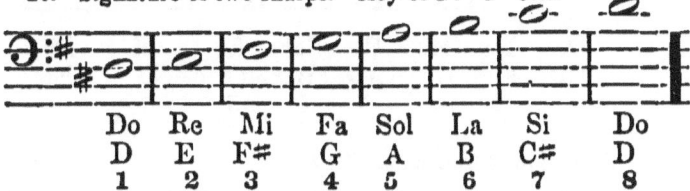

17. Signature of three sharps. Key of A.

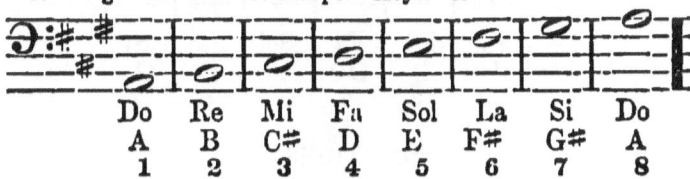

18. Signature of four sharps. Key of E.

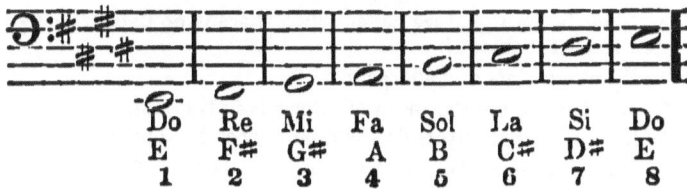

19. Signature of one flat. Key of F.

20. Signature of two flats. Key of Bb.

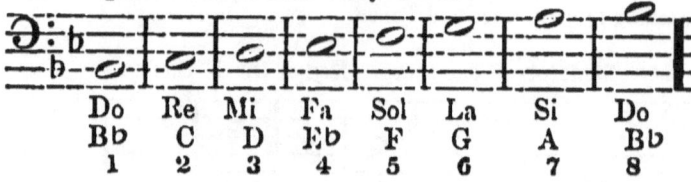

21. Signature of three flats. Key of Eb.

22. Signature of four flats. Key of Ab.

QUESTIONS.

1. When is the scale transposed?
2. When is it in its natural position?
3. What is the signature called when there is no flats or sharps at the commencement?
4. What are flats and sharps used for?
5. What is the regular order of intervals in the scale?
6. Between what letters do the minor seconds occur?
7. If the signature be one sharp, on what letter is 1?

8. If the signature be two sharps on what letter is 1?
9. Three sharps?
10. Four sharps?
11. One flat?
12. Two flats?
13. Three flats?
14. Four flats?

NOTE. The teacher must be very careful to make each one understand the scale, and all the different keys, for if the learner do not understand the use of flats, sharps, and naturals most thoroughly, they can never read music correctly. The space in a work like this will not permit us to take up the subject in that slow and *progressive* manner which every good teacher might wish to use. Let him be very careful to explain all the intervals in the scale, in all the different keys, being always careful to impress on the mind, the position of the minor seconds in the scale, and that the intervals are always the same in *tunes*, as in *scales* with the *same signature*.

LESSON TENTH.

CHROMATIC SCALE.

1. Between those sounds of the scale which are a major second distant from each other, intermediate sounds may occur.
2. There can be no sound between those sounds which are only a minor second distant from each other, for there is no smaller practicable interval than the minor second.
3. The notes representing intermediate sounds may be written on the same degree of the staff with either of the sounds between which they occur, as the following example will show.

4. In the application of the syllables to the sharped sounds, the vowel sound is changed to ee. Thus, Do♯ is di, (pronounced dee,) Re♯, ri, &c.

[2*]

5. In the application of syllables to the flatted sounds, the vowel sound is changed to *a*, (a as in day.) Thus, Si♭ is *sa*.

6. A scale of thirteen sounds, including all the intermediate sounds, and twelve intervals of a minor second each, is called the Chromatic scale; thus:

THE CHROMATIC SCALE.

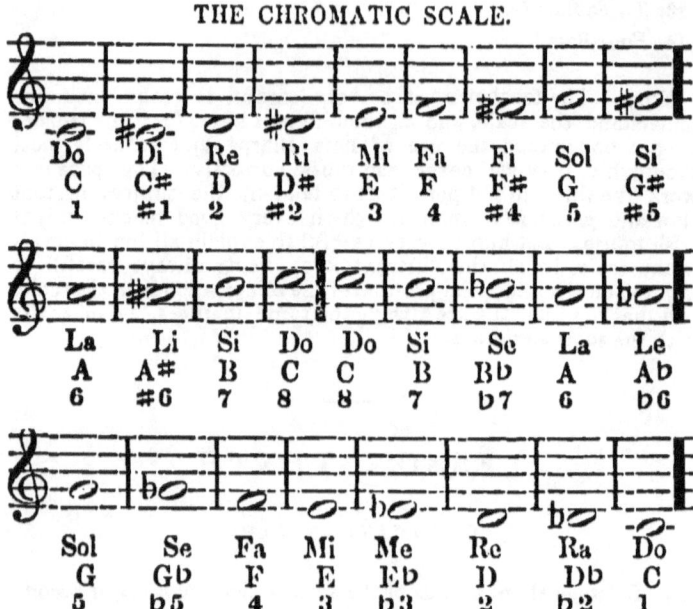

7. A flat, or sharp (used as an accidental,) affects all notes coming after it on the letter on which it is placed throughout the measure in which it is used.

8. A sharp, flat, or natural occurring in a piece of music, in any other place than as a signature, is called an Accidental.

9. When a flatted or sharped note is continued from one measure to another on the same degree of the staff, the influence of the flat or sharp is continued, as the following example will illustrate.

EXAMPLE OF ACCIDENTALS.

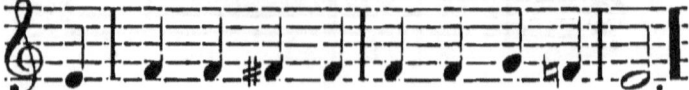

10. When it is desirable to contradict a flat or sharp, or to take away the effect of either of those characters, a character called a natural is used, as above.

ELEMENTS OF MUSIC.   19

QUESTIONS.

1. Between what parts of the scale may intermediate sounds occur?
2. Between which parts of the scale can there be no intermediate sounds?
3. How can we write the intermediate notes?
4. In the application of syllables to the sharped sounds, what vowel-sound is used?
5. In the application of syllables to the flatted sounds, what vowel sound is used?
6. How many sounds in the Chromatic scale?
7. An accidental flat or sharp affects how many notes?
8. What is an accidental?
9. When a flatted or sharped note is continued from one measure to another, what can you say of the influence of the flat or sharp?
10. What do we use to contradict a flat or sharp?

LESSON ELEVENTH.

THE MINOR SCALE.

1. Besides the Major, and the Chromatic scales already given, we have another, called the Minor scale.
2. The order of intervals in the Minor scale, is different from that in the Major scale.
3. There are several forms of the Minor scale.
4. The difference in these forms consists in the order of intervals being different.
5. Each Major scale has its relative Minor.
6. The Minor scale in its natural position, commences on A, as the following examples will illustrate.

MINOR SCALE OF A, ASCENDING.

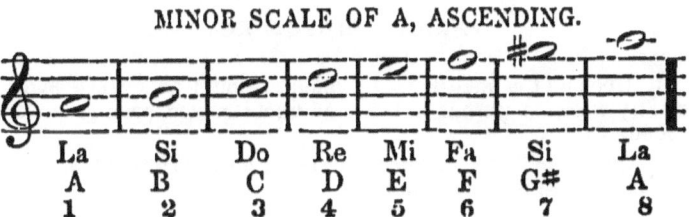

La	Si	Do	Re	Mi	Fa	Si	La
A	B	C	D	E	F	G#	A
1	2	3	4	5	6	7	8

MINOR SCALE OF A, DESCENDING.

La	Si	Fa	Mi	Re	Do	Si	La
A	G#	F	E	D	C	B	A
8	7	6	5	4	3	2	1

NOTE. It is deemed unnecessary to explain any other form of the minor scale here, for any person who can sing the form here given, and the Chromatic scale, will find no difficulty in any form of the minor scale.

7. The example above, is the relative minor of C major.
8. The letters and syllables always correspond in the major and its relative minor.

QUESTIONS.

1. What scale have we, beside the Major and Chromatic?
2. What is the difference between the Major and Minor scale?
3. Is there more than one form of the Minor scale?
4. What is the difference in these forms?
5. What is said of the relation of scales?
6. What letter does the relative minor of C major commence on?
8. What always corresponds between the Major and relative Minor scales?

NOTE. The teacher will here explain the Major, and Minor seconds, and also the Augmented second between six and seven in the above scales.

LESSON TWELFTH.

VARIOUS DIRECTIONS.

1. **Opening the mouth.** The mouth should be opened sufficiently wide, to permit a free and unobstructed passage of the sound.
2. **Quality of Tone.** A tone to be good, must be firm, pure, full, and made with much certainty.

ELEMENTS OF MUSIC. 21

3. Emphasis. Emphatic words should be given with as much power, as in reading or speaking.

4. Taking breath. As little noise as possible should be made in taking breath.

5. It should be done very quickly, without changing the position of the mouth.

6. Never take breath between two syllables of the same word.

7. Do not spoil the sense of the language by taking breath in the middle of a sentence, where it would not be allowed in reading

8. Do not take breath too often.

LESSON THIRTEENTH.

EMBELLISHMENT.

1. A turn consists of a principal sound with the sounds next above and below it. Some of the forms of writing and performing of which, are as follows:

2. The shake is generally used on the last note but one of a musical phrase.

3. It is produced by the quick and equal performance of a principal note, and the note above, and terminated by a turn formed of the next note below the principal note, and the principal note itself.

The following examples will illustrate some of the different forms of the shake.

4. *Passing Note.* Ornamental or grace notes are often used that do not essentially belong to the Melody.

5. They are generally written in small characters, and are called Passing Notes.

6. When the passing note precedes the essential note, it is called an Appoggiatura, and is written and performed as follows:

APPOGGIATURAS DESCENDING.

APPOGGIATURAS ASCENDING.

7. When the passing note follows the essential note, it is called an after note, written and performed thus:

AFTER NOTES.

QUESTIONS.

1. Of what does a turn consist?
2. On what note is the shake commonly used?
3. How is it produced?
4. What is said of the passing note?
5. How are they written?
6. What is it called when it precedes the essential note?
7. When it follows the essential note, what is it called?

EXPLANATION OF MUSICAL TERMS.

Adagio. Signifies the slowest time.
Ad libitum, or *Ad lib.* At pleasure.
Affetuoso. In a style of execution adapted to express affection, tenderness, supplication, and deep emotion.
Allegro. Very quick.
Allegretto. Less quick than Allegro.
Alto. The part next the air.
Amoroso. In a soft and delicate style.
Andante. With distinctness, and rather slow.
Andantino. Quicker than Andante.
Anthem. A musical composition set to sacred prose.
A tempo. In time. (used after a retarded passage.)
Bass. The lowest part in harmony.
Bis. Twice, or repeat.
Chorus. All the parts, or voices.
Coda. The Close, or an additional Close.
Da Capo, or *D. C.* Close with the first strain.
Del Segno, or *Al Segno.* From the sign.
Dirge. A piece composed for funeral occasions.
Duett, or *Duo.* Consisting of two parts.
Dolce. Sweetness, softness, gentleness, &c.
Expressivo. With expression.
Fine. The end.
Forte, or *f.* Strong, or loud.
Fortissimo, or *ff.* Very loud.
Guisto. In a steady, equal, and just time.
Grazioso. In a soft, smooth, and gentle style.
Harmony. An agreeable combination of musical sounds.
Interval. The difference between any two notes.
Interlude. An instrumental passage introduced between two vocal passages.
Largo. Pretty slow.
Legato. Slurring the notes together.

EXPLANATION OF MUSICAL TERMS.

Lento. Slow.
Lentando. Gradually retarding.
Melody. The highest part, or air.
Mezzo. Half.
Moderato. Moderately.
Orchestra. The place for, or a band of musicians.
Piano, or *pia,* or *p.* Soft.
Pianissimo, or *pp.* Very soft.
Presto. Quick.
Primo. The first part.
Quartetto. A composition of four parts.
Quintetto. A composition of five parts.
Rallentando. To diminish the time and sound gradually.
Recitative. A sort of musical declamation, having to each syllable a musical sound.
Ritard, or *Ritardando.* Slackening the time by degrees.
Semi Chorus. Half the choir, or voices.
Soave. Soft.
Solo. For a single voice.
Soli. For single voices in the parts.
Soprano. The treble, or higher female voices.
Spirituoso. With spirit.
Staccato. Short and distinct.
Tempo. In time.
Tenor. A high male voice, or the part next the bass in harmony.
Treble. The highest female voices, or the **melody.**
Trio. A composition of three parts.
Tutti. All together.
Un poco. A little.
Unison. Notes on the same letter.
Vivace. A quick movement.
Voce di petto. Chest voice.
Voce di testa. Head voice.
Vigoroso. Strong, vigorous.

PRACTICAL EXERCISES.

PRACTICAL EXERCISES. 27

PRACTICAL EXERCISES. 29

LESSON IN 2 PARTS.

No. 11.

TRIO FOR TREBLE VOICES.

No. 12.

[3*]

PRACTICAL EXERCISES.

DUETT.   RANSOM.
No. 13.

'Tis finished! now the ran-som's paid,

Re-ceive my soul, ... he ...... cries;

Be-hold he bows his sa-cred head;

He bows his head and dies.

PRACTICAL EXERCISES.   31

OLD HUNDRED. No. 2.

No. 14.   Trio for Trebles.

A CHORAL FOR THREE TREBLE PARTS.

No. 15.

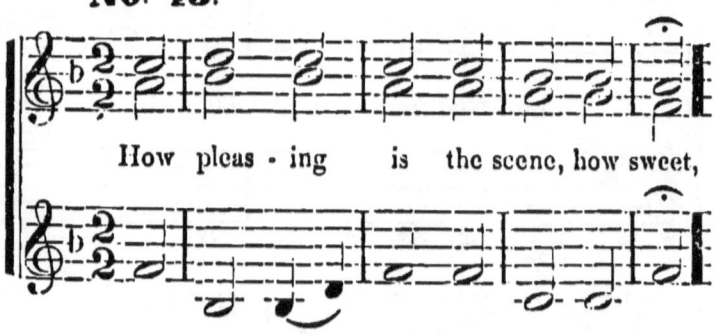

How pleas - ing is the scene, how sweet,

Where Christian souls in friend - ship join;

Whose cares, and joys, u - ni - ted meet,

PRACTICAL EXERCISES. 33

In bonds of char - i - ty di - vine.

No. 16. Duett.

PRACTICAL EXERCISES.

WELLS.

No. 17.

Life is the time to serve the Lord,
The time t' in-sure the great reward;
And while the lamp holds out to burn,
The vi-lest sin-ner may re-turn.

WILLIAMS.

G. J. WEBB.

No. 19.

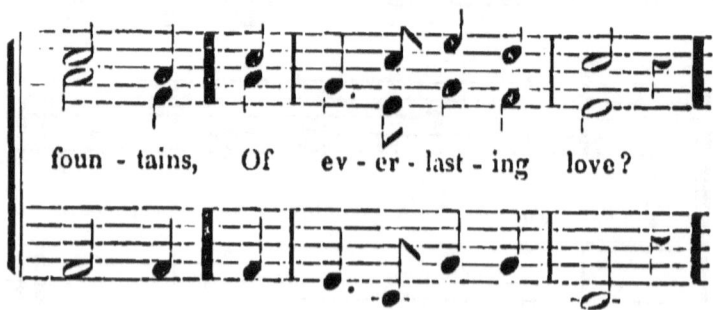

PRACTICAL EXERCISES. 37

[¼]

ARNOLD. L. M.

DR. ARNOLD.

1. Prayer is ap-pointed to con-vey The bless-ings
2. If pain af-flict, or wrongs op-press; If cares dis-
3. 'Tis pray'r supports the soul that's weak: Tho' thought be
4. De-pend on him: thou canst not fail; Make all thy

God de-signs to give; Long as they live should Christians
tract, or fears dis-may; If guilt de-ject; if sin dis-
broken, lan-guage lame, Pray, if thou canst or can-not
wants and wish-es known; Fear not; his mer-its must pre-

pray; They learn to pray when first they live.
tress; In eve-ry case, still watch and pray.
speak; But pray with faith in Je-sus' name.
vail: Ask but in faith, it shall be done.

CLEAVELAND. L. M.
From the "Sacred Choir."

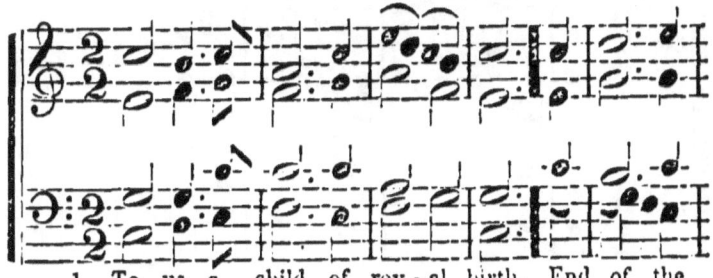

1. To us a child of roy-al birth, End of the prom-i-ses, is giv'n; The In- -visi-ble ap-pears on earth,—The Son of man, the God of heaven.
2. A Saviour born, in love su-preme, He comes, our fal-len souls to raise; He comes, his peo-ple to re-deem, With all his plen-i-tude of grace.
3. The Christ, by raptur'd seers fore-told, Fill'd with the Ho-ly Spir-it's pow'r, Proph-et, and Priest, and King be-hold; And Lord of all the worlds a-bove.
4. The Lord of hosts, the God most high, Who quits his throne, on earth to live, With joy we wel-come from the sky, With faith in-to our hearts re-ceive

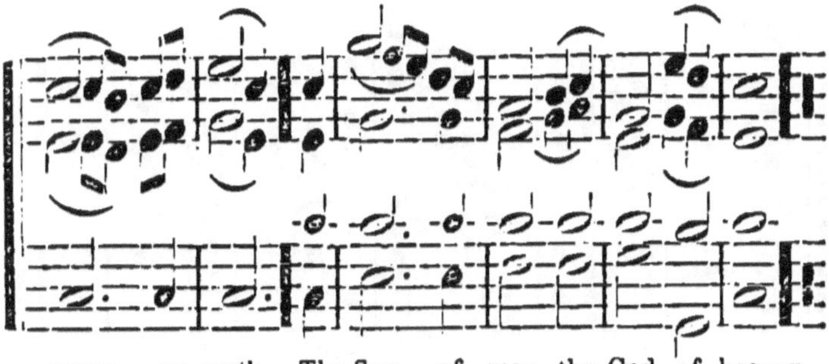

NEW SABBATH. L. M. — SMITH.

1. A-rise, my soul, on wings sub-lime, A-
2. Born by a new, ce-les-tial birth, Why
3. Shall aught be-guile me on the road—The
4. To dwell with God— to taste his love Is

bove the van - - i - - ties of time; Let faith now pierce the
should I gro - vel here on earth? Why grasp at vain and
nar row road that leads to God? Or can I love this
the full heav'n en - joyed above: The glo - rious ex-pec-

veil and see The glo - ries of e - ter - ni - ty.
fleet - ing toys, So near to heaven's e - ter - nal joys?
earth so well, As not to long with God to dwell?
ta - tion now Is heaven-ly bliss be - gun be - low.

MENDON. L. M.

1. God, in the gos-pel of his Son, Makes his e-
2. Here sin-ners of an hum-ble frame May taste his
3. Here Je-sus, in ten thou-sand ways, His soul-at-
4. Wis-dom its dic-tates here im-parts, To form our

ter-nal coun-sels known; 'Tis here his rich-est mer-cy
grace and learn his name; 'Tis shown in char-ac-ters of
tract-ing charms dis-plays: Recounts his pov-er-ty and
minds, to cheer our hearts; Its influence makes the sin-ner

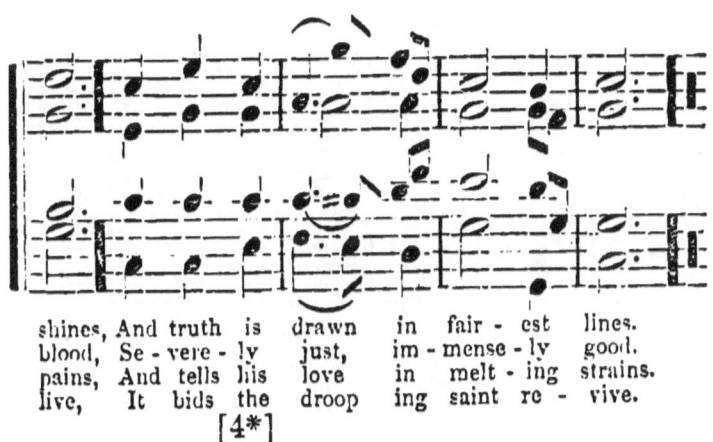

shines, And truth is drawn in fair-est lines.
blood, Se-vere-ly just, im-mense-ly good.
pains, And tells his love in melt-ing strains.
live, It bids the droop ing saint re-vive.

[4*]

ALL SAINTS. L. M.

Arranged from WM. KNAPP.

1. 'Tis by the faith of joys to come, We
2. The want of sight she well sup-plies, She
3. Cheer-ful we tread the des-ert through, While
4. So Abra'm, by di-vine command, Left

walk thro' des-erts dark as night; Till we ar-rive at
makes the pear-ly gates ap-pear; Far in-to dis-tant
faith in-spires a heavenly ray, Tho' li-ons roar, and
his own house to walk with God: His faith be-held the

heaven, our home, Faith is our guide, and faith our light.
worlds she pries, And brings e-ter-nal glo-ries near.
tempests blow, And rocks and dan-gers fill the way.
promised land; And fired his zeal a-long the road

 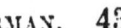

MUNICH. L. M.   GERMAN.

1. " 'Tis finished!" 'tis fin-ished! so the Saviour cried,
2. 'Tis fin-ished! 'tis finished! this his dying groan,
3. 'Tis fin-ished! 'tis fin-ished! Heaven is reconciled,
4. 'Tis fin-ished! 'tis fin-ished! let the joy-ful sound

And meekly bowed his head and died; 'Tis finished! yes, the
Shall sins of deepest hue a-tone, And millions be re-
And all the powers of dark-ness spoiled; Peace, love, and happi
Be heard thro' all the na-tions round; 'Tis finished! let the

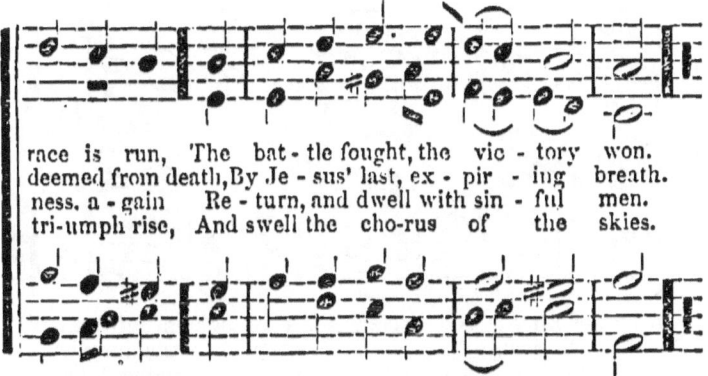

race is run, The bat-tle fought, the vic-tory won.
deemed from death, By Je-sus' last, ex-pir-ing breath.
ness. a-gain Re-turn, and dwell with sin-ful men.
tri-umph rise, And swell the cho-rus of the skies.

* From the New York Choralist, by permission.

RAYMOND. L. M.

1. Glo-ry to thee, my God this night, For all the
2. Forgive me, Lord, for thy dear Son, The ill which
3. Teach me to live, that I may dread The grave as
4. O let my soul on thee re-pose, And may sweet

bless-ings of the light; Keep me, O keep me,
I...... this day have done; That with the world, my-
lit-tle as my bed; Teach me to die,.... that
sleep mine eye-lids close; Sleep which shall me more

King of kings, Be-neath the shad-ow of thy wings.
-self and thee, I, ere I sleep, at peace may be.
so.... I may Rise glo-rious at the judgment day.
vig'-rous make, To serve my God, when I a-wake.

GRATITUDE. L. M. NICOLAI. 45

1. Not diff'rent food, nor diff'rent dress, Compose the
2. When weaker Christians we des-pise, We do the
3. Let pride and wrath be banish'd hence; Meekness and
4. Then we who own one Father here, And walk in

king - dom of our Lord; But peace, and joy, and
gos - pel migh - ty wrong; For God, the gracious
love our souls pur - sue; Nor shall our patience
meek - ness and in love, Shall 'round his board in

righteous - ness, Faith, and o - be-dience to his word.
and the wise, Re - ceives the fee - ble with the strong.
give of - fence To saints, the Gentile, or the Jew.
heaven ap - pear, And form one broth-er - hood a - bove.

HAMNER. L. M.

1 O praise the Lord in that blest place From whence his
2 Praise him for all the migh-ty acts Which he in
3 Let the shrill trumpet's war-like voice Make rocks and
4 Let them who joyful hymns compose, To cym-bals
5 Let all that vi-tal breath en-joy, The breath he

good-ness large-ly flows: Praise him in heaven, where
our be-half has done; His kindness this re-
hills his praise re-bound; Praise him with harp's me-
set their songs of praise; To well-tuned cymbals,
does to them af-ford, In just re-turns of

he his face, Unveil'd, in perfect glo-ry shows.
-turn ex-acts, With which our praise should equal run.
-lo-dious noise, And gentle psaltery's silver sound.
and to those That loudly sound on solemn days.
prais e employ: Let every creature praise the Lord!

HEBRON. L. M.   HANDEL.

1. Ere mountains rear'd their forms sublime, Or heaven and
2. A thousand ages, in their flight, With thee are
3. But our brief life's a shadowy dream, A pass-ing
4. To us, O Lord, the wisdom give, Each pass-ing

earth in or-der stood, Be-fore the birth of
as a fleeting day; Past, pres-ent, fu-ture,
thought, that soon is o'er, That fades with morning's
mo-ment so to speed, That we at length with

an-cient time, From ev-er-last-ing thou art God.
to thy sight At once their va-rious scenes dis-play.
ear-liest beam, And fills the mus-ing mind no more
thee may live Where life and bliss shall nev-er end.

SABAOTH. L. M.
W. TAYLOR.

1. Saints, at your heavenly Father's word, Give up your
2. So Abra'am, with o-bedient hand, Led forth his
3. 'Abra'am, for-bear,' the an-gel cry'd, 'Thy faith is
4. Just in the last distress-ing hour, The Lord dis

comforts to the Lord; He will restore what you re-
son, at God's com-mand: The wood, the fire, the knife he
known, thy love is try'd, Thy son shall live, and in thy
plays de-liv'-ring power; The mount of danger is the

-sign, 'Or grant you bless-ings more di-vine.
took, His arm pre-pared the dread-ful stroke.
seed Shall the whole earth be bless'd in-deed.'
place, Where we shall see sur-pris-ing grace.

VALENTIA. L. M. READ. 49

1. Ex - tend - ed on a curs - ed tree, Cov -
2. Who, who, my Sa - viour, this hath done? Who
3. I, I a - lone have done the deed; 'Tis
4. My Saviour, how shall I pro - claim, How

er'd with dust, and sweat, and blood, See there, the King of
could thy sa - cred bod - y wound? No guilt thy spotless
I thy sa - cred flesh have torn; My sins have caused thee,
pay the might - y debt I owe? Let all I have, and

glo - ry, see! Sinks and expires the son of God.
heart has known, No guile hath in thy lips been found.
Lord, to bleed, Point - ed the nail, and fixed the thorn.
all I am, Ceaseless, to all, thy glo - ry show.

[5]

EL PARAN. L. M.

Arranged from MOZART.

1. Thou Lamb of God, thou Prince of peace. For thee my
2. With fraudless, e - ven, humble mind, Thy will in
3. When pain o'er my weak flesh prevails, With lamb-like
4. Close by thy side still may I keep, Howe'er life's

thirs - ty soul doth pine; My long - ing heart im - plores thy
all things may I see; In love be ev' - ry wish re
pa - tience arm my breast: When grief my wounded soul as
va - rious cur-rent flow'; With stead-fast eye mark ev' - ry

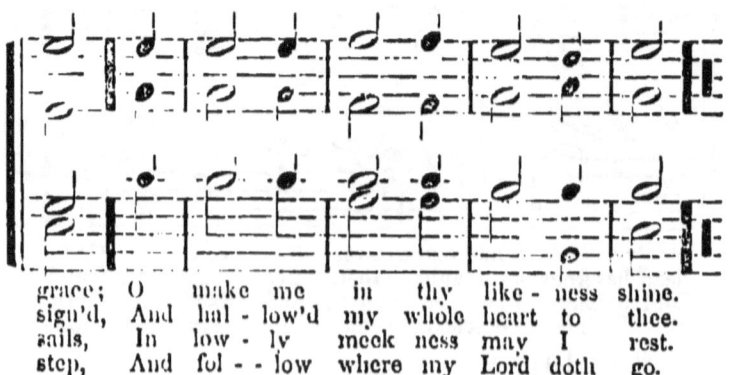

grace; O make me in thy like - ness shine.
sign'd, And hal - low'd my whole heart to thee.
sails, In low - ly meek ness may I rest.
step, And fol - - low where my Lord doth go.

SOUTH STREET. L. M.

Arranged from HAYDN.

1. Fath-er of men, thy care we bless, Which crowns our
2. To God most wor-thy to be prais'd, Be our do-
3. To thee may each u-nit-ed House, Morn-ing and
4. Oh may each fu-ture age pro-claim The hon-ors

fam-i-lies with peace; From thee they sprung, and by thy
mes-tic al-tars rais'd; Who, Lord of Heaven, scorn not to
night, pre-sent its vows; Our ser-vants here, and ris ing
of thy glo-rious name; While, pleas'd and thankful, we re-

hand Their roots and branch-es are sus-tain'd.
dwell With saints in their ob--scur-est cell.
race, Be taught thy pre--cepts, and thy grace.
move, To join the fam-i-ly a--bove.

TEMPLE STREET. L. M.

Arranged from PLEYEL.

1. Blest are the hum-ble souls who see Their empti
2. Blest are the men of brok-en heart, Who mourn for
3. Blest are the meek, who stand a - far, From rage and
4. Blest are the souls that thirst for grace, Hunger and

ness and pov - - er - ty: Treasures of grace to them are
sins with in - ward smart; The blood of Christ di - vine - ly
pas - sion, noise and war; God will se - cure their hap - py
long for right - eousness; They shall be well supplied and

given, And crowns of joy laid up in heaven.
flows, A heal - ing balm for all their woes.
state, And plead their cause a - gainst the great.
fed With liv ing streams and liv - ing bread.

WINDHAM. L. M. READ. 53

1. 'Tis mid-night, and on Ol-ive's brow, The
2. 'Tis mid-night, and from all re-moved, In-
3. 'Tis mid-night, and for oth-ers' guilt The
4. 'Tis mid-night, and from e-ther plains, Is

star is dim'd that late-ly shone; 'Tis midnight, in the
man-uel wrest-les lone with fears; E'en the dis-ci-ple
man of sor-rows weeps in blood; Yet he that hath in
borne the songs that an-gels know; Un-heard by mor-tals

gar-den now, The suff'ring Sa-vior prays a-lone.
that he lov'd Heeds not his Mas-ter's grief and tears
an-guish knelt, Is not for-sak-en by his God.
are the strains, That sweetly soothe the Sa-viour's wo.

[5*]

WISDOM. L. M.

Arranged from ROTTER. By permission.

1. He reigns, the Lord the Saviour reigns: Praise
2. Deep are his counsels, and unknown; But
3. In robes of judgment, lo, he comes! Shakes
4. His enemies, with sore dismay, Fly

him in evangelic strains: Let the whole earth in
grace and truth support his throne: Tho' gloomy clouds his
the wide earth and cleaves the tombs: Before him burns de-
from the sight and shun the day: Then lift your heads, ye

songs rejoice; And distant islands join their voice.
ways surround, Justice is their eternal ground.
vouring fire! The mountains melt, the seas retire.
saints on high, And sing, for your redemption's nigh.

CLINTON. L. M.
LEACH. 55

1. Je-sus, and shall it ev-er be, A mor-tal
2. Ashamed of Je-sus! that dear Friend, On whom my
3. Ashamed of Je-sus! yes I may, When I've no
4. Till then, nor is my boast-ing vain, Till then I

man a-shamed of thee? Ashamed of thee, whom an-gels
hopes of heaven de-pend; No! when I blush, be this my
guilt to wash a-way; No tear to wipe, no good to
boast a Sa-viour slain; And, O may this my glo-ry

praise, Whose glo - ries shine thro' end - less days.
shame, That I no more re - vere his name.
crave, No fears to quell, no soul to save.
be, That Christ is not a - shamed of me.

HINGHAM. L. M. CARY.

1. Sweet is the work, my God, my King, To praise thy name, give
2. Sweet is the day of sa-cred rest; No mortal cares shall
3. When grace has pu-ri-fied my heart, Then I shall share a
4. Then shall I see, and hear, and know All I desired or

Organ.

thanks and sing; To show thy love by morning light, And talk of
seize my breast; O may my heart in tune be found, Like David's
glorious part; And fresh supplies of joy be shed, Like ho-ly
wish'd be-low; And every power find sweet employ In that e-

all thy truths by night, And talk of all thy truths by night.
harp of solemn sound, Like David's harp of sol-emn sound.
oil to cheer my head, Like ho-ly oil to cheer my head.
ternal world of joy, In that e-ter-nal world of joy.

ROCKINGHAM. L. M.

Arranged from W. DIXON.

1. To us the voice of Wisdom cries, 'Hearken, ye
2. Happy the man who dai - ly waits To hear me
3. To them that love me I am kind, And those who
4. Mark the be - gin ning of my law, Fear ye the

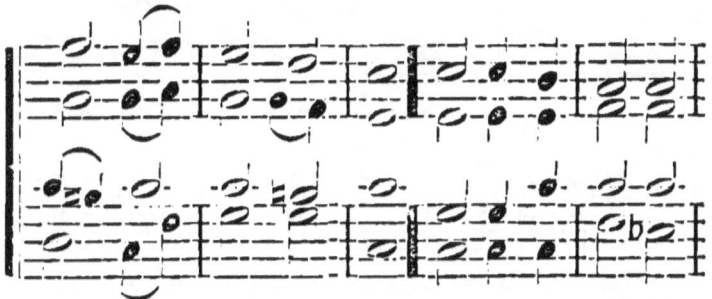

chil - dren, and be wise; Better than gold the
watch - ing at my gates; Wretched is he who
seek me ear - ly, find; My son, give me thine
Lord with sa - cred awe: Mark the ful fil - ment

fruit I bear, Rubies with me may not com - pare.
scorns my voice, Death and destruc - tion are his choice.
heart, and learn Wisdom from fol - ly to dis - cern.
of the whole, Love ye the Lord with all your soul.'

BATTEE. L. M.

A. J. CLEAVELAND.

1. Ye nations of the earth re-joice, Be-
2. The Lord is God;— 'tis he a-lone Doth
3. En-ter his gates with songs of joy; With
4. The Lord is good; the Lord is kind; Great

fore the Lord, your sov'reign King, Serve him with cheer-ful
life and breath and be-ing give; We are his work, and
praises to his courts re-pair; And make it your di
is his grace, his mer-cy sure; And the whole race of

heart and voice: With all your tongues his glory sing.
not our own; The sheep that on his pasture live.
vine employ, To pay your thanks and honors there.
man shall find His truth from age to age endure.

MALAN. L. M.

1. Why should we start, and fear to die? What tim'rous worms we mortals are! Death is the gate to endless joy, And yet we dread to enter there.
2. The pains, the groans, the dying strife, Fright our approaching souls away; And we shrink back again to life, Fond of our prison and our clay.
3. O would my Lord his servant meet, My soul would stretch her wings in haste, Fly fearless through death's iron gate, Nor feel the terrors as she pass'd.
4. Jesus can make a dying bed Feel soft as downy pillows are, When on his breast I lean my head, And breathe my life out sweetly there.

SAXTON. L. M. — COLLIER

1. Eter-nal pow'r, whose high abode   Becomes the
2. Thee while the first arch-angel sings,   He hides his
3. Lord, what shall earth and ashes do?   We would a-
4. Earth from a-far, hath heard thy fame, And worms have

grandeur of   a   God: In - finite lengths beyond   the
face be-hind   his wings;   And ranks of shining thrones a-
dore our Maker   too;   From sin and dust to   thee   we
learn'd to lisp thy name: But O! the glo-ries   of   thy

bounds Where stars re - volve their lit - tle rounds.
- round Fall wor - ship - ping, and spread the ground.
cry, The Great, the Ho - ly and the High.
mind Leave all   our   soar ing thoughts be - hind.

DUDLEY. L. M. COLSON. 61

1. Life and im-mor-tal joys are given To souls that
2. Wo to the wretch who never felt The inward
3. The law condemns the rebel dead; Un-der the
4. Then turn to God; with tears and shame In pen-i-

mourn the sins they've done; Children of wrath, made
pangs of pi-ous grief; But adds to all his
wrath of God he lies: He seals the curse on
tence your sins con-fess; Be-liev-ing on the

heirs of heav'n, By faith in God's e-ter-nal Son.
crying guilt The stubborn sin of un-be lief.
his own head, And with a double vengeance dies.
Saviour's name With willing heart of right-eous-ness.

[6]

DRESDEN. L. M. D. NAUMAN.

1. He dies! the Friend of sinners dies! Lo, Salem's
2. Here's love and grief beyond degree: The Lord of
3. Break off your tears, ye saints, and tell How high your

daughters weep a-round; A sol-emn dark-ness
glo-ry . dies for man! But lo! what sud-den
great De liv'-rer reigns; Sing how he spoiled the

veils the skies, A sud-den trembling shakes the ground
joys we see: Je-sus, the dead, re-vives a-gain.
hosts of hell, And led the mon-ster death in chains

63

Come, saints, and drop a tear or two For him who
The ris-ing God forsakes the tomb; (In vain the
Say, Live for-ev-er, wondrous King! Borne to re

groan'd beneath your load; He shed a thousand
tomb for-bids his rise:) Cher-u-bic le-gions
deem, and strong to save; Then ask the mon-ster,

drops for you, A thousand drops of rich-er blood.
guard him home, And shout him wel-come to the skies.
Where's thy sting? And, Where's thy vict'ry, boasting grave?

WARE. L. M.
DEA. N. D. GOULD.

1. Je - sus, we on thy word de - pend, Spok-
2. That promise made to Ad - am's race, Now,
3. That heavenly Teach-er of man-kind, That
4. He on - ly can the words ap - ply, Through

en by thee while pre - sent here, The Fa - ther in my
Lord, in us we pray, ful - fil And give the Spi - rit
Guide in-fal - li - ble, im - part, To bring thy say - ings
which we endless life pos - sess; And deal to each his

name shall send The Ho-ly Ghost, the Com - fort - er.
of thy grace, To teach us all thy per - fect will.
to our mind, And write them on each faith - ful heart.
leg - a - cy, Our Lord's un-ut - ter - a - ble peace.

ALFRETON. L. M.

1. Now in the heat of youthful blood, Re-
2. Be-hold the a-ged sin-ner goes, La-
3. The dust re-turns to dust a-gain; The
4. E-ter-nal King, I fear thy name! Teach

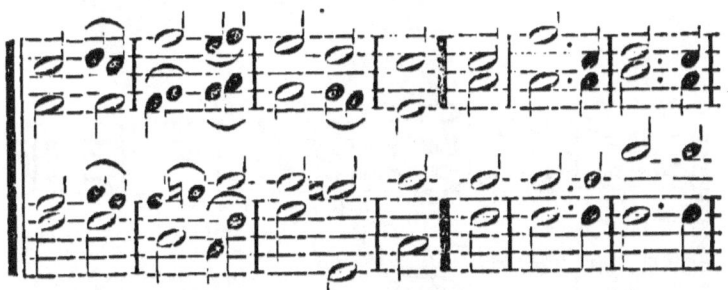

mem-ber your Cre-a-tor, God; Behold the months come
den with guilt and heav-y woes, Down to the re-gions
soul, in ag-o-nies of pain, As-cends to God; not
me to know how frail I am; And when my soul must

hast'-ning on, When you shall say, My joys are gone.
of the dead, With end-less curs-es on his head.
there to dwell, But hears her doom, and sinks to hell.
hence re-move, Give me a man-sion in thy love.

[6*]

SARGENT. L. M. DOUBLE.

From the "Creation."

1. He who hath made his ref - uge—God, Shall
2. If burn-ing beams of noon con - spire To

find a most se - cure a - bode; Shall walk all day be-
dart a pes - ti - len - tial fire, God is their life: his

neath his shade, And there at night shall rest his head.
wings are spread, To shield them with a healthful shade.

Then will I say, 'My God thy pow'r, Shall
If va-pors, with ma--lig-nant breath, Rise

be my for-tress and my tow'r: I, that am form'd of
thick and scat-ter mid-night death, Is-ra-el is safe:

fee-ble dust, Make thine al-migh-ty arm my trust.
the poison'd air Grows pure, if Is-rael's God be there.

WAREFIELD. L. M. SHOEL.

1. Be-hold the Christian war-rior stand In
2. In pan-o-ply of truth com-plete, Sal-
3. Un-dannt-ed to the field he goes; Yet
4. Thus, strong in his Re-deem-er's strength, Sin,

all the ar-mor of his God: The Spir it's sword is
va-tion's hel-met on his head; With righteousness a
vain were skill and val-or there, Un-less to foil his
death, and hell, he tram-ples down; Fights the good fight and

in his hand, His feet are with the gos-pel shod.
breast-plate meet, And faith's broad shield be-fore him spread.
le-gion foes, He takes the trust-iest weapon, prayer.
wins at length, Thro' mer-cy an im-mortal crown.

OLD HUNDRED. L. M.

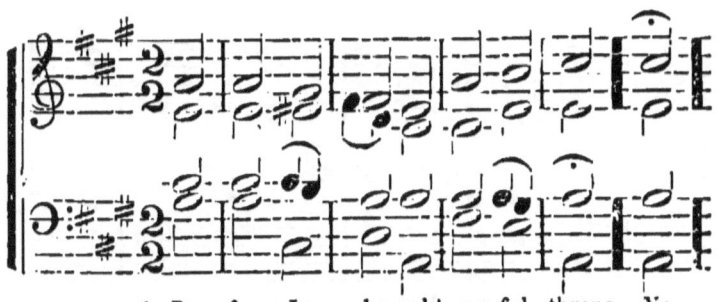

1. Be-fore Je-ho-vah's aw-ful throne, Ye
2. His sov'reign pow'r without our aid, Made
3. We'll crowd thy gates with thankful songs, High
4. Wide as the world is thy command; Vast

na-tions bow with sa-cred joy; Know that the Lord is
us of clay, and form'd us men; And when like wand'ring
as the heav'ns our voi-ces raise; And earth with her ten
as e - - ter - ni-ty they love; Firm as a rock thy

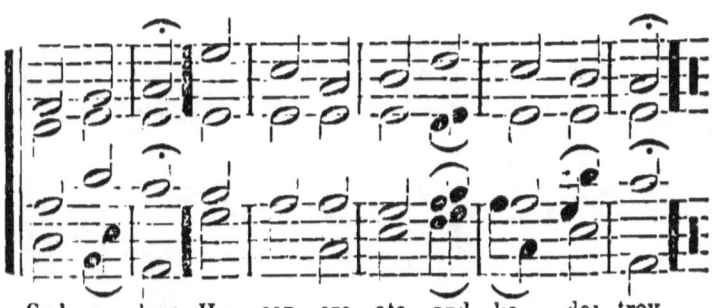

God a-lone, He can cre-ate, and he des-troy.
sheep we stray'd, He brought us to his fold a-gain.
thou-sand tongues, Shall fill thy courts with sound-ing praise.
truth shall stand, When roll-ing years shall cease to move.

BROOKLYN. L. M. — DR. C. BURNEY.

1. Wisdom di-vine! who tells the price Of wisdom's
2. Her hands are fill'd with length of days, True riches.
3. To purest joys she all invites,—Chaste, ho-ly.
4. Happy the man who wisdom gains; Thrice happy,

cost - ly merchan - dise? Wis - dom to sil - ver
and im - mor - tal praise, Rich - es of Christ on
spir - it - ual de - lights; Her ways are ways of
who his guest re - tains; He owns, and shall for -

we pre - fer, And gold is dross compared to her.
all be - stow'd, And hon - or that descends from God.
pleasant - ness, And all her flowery paths are peace.
ev - er own, Wisdom, and Christ, and heaven are one.

HAMBURG. L. M. GREGORIAN.

1. Ye that pass by, be-hold the Man-
2. His sa-cred limbs they stretch, they tear;
3. Be-hold his tem-ples, crown'd with thorn;
4. O thou dear suff'-ring Son of God,

The Man of griefs, condemn'd for you; The Lamb of God for
With nails they fasten to the wood; His sacred limbs ex-
His bleeding hands, extend-ed wide; His streaming feet, trans-
How doth thy heart to sinners move; Sprinkle on us thy

sin-ners slain, Weeping to Cal-va-ry pur-sue;
posed and bare, Or on-ly cov-er'd with his blood.
fix'd and torn; The fountain gushing from his side!
pre-cious blood, And melt us with thy dy-ing love.

COMPASSION. L. M.
N. D. GOULD.

1. Lord, we be-lieve to us and ours The
2. As-sem-bled here with one ac-cord, Calm-
3. If ev-ry one that asks may find,— If
4. Ah! leave us not to mourn be-low, Or

a-pos-tol-ic promise given; We wait the pen - te-
-ly we wait the promised grace, The purchase of our
still thou dost on sin-ners fall,— Come as a migh - ty
long for thy return to pine; Now, Lord, the Com - fort-

-cos-tal powers,— The Ho-ly Ghost sent down from heaven.
dy-ing Lord; Come, Ho-ly Ghost, and fill the place.
rush-ing wind; Great grace be now up-on us all.
-er bestow, And fix in us the Guest divine.

DUKE STREET. L. M.
J. HATTON.

1. Bless'd be the Fa-ther and his love, To which ce-
2. Glo-ry to thee, great Son of God, From whose dear
3. We give thee, sa-cred Spir-it, praise, Who in our
4. Thus God the Fa-ther, God the Son, And God the

- les-tial source we owe Rivers of end-less
wounded bod-y rolls A precious stream of
hearts of sin and wo, Mak'st living springs of
Spir-it, we a-dore; The sea of life and

joy a-bove, And rills of com-fort here be-low.
vi-tal blood, Pardon and life...... for dy-ing souls!
grace a-rise, And in-to bound-less glo-ry flow.
love unknown, Without a bot-tom or a shore.

[7]

THORPE. L. M.

A. J. CLEAVELAND.

1. From every stormy wind that blows, From
2. There is a place where Je - sus sheds The
3. There is a scene, where spir - its blend, Where
4. There, there on eagle's wings we soar, And

every swelling tide of woes, There is a calm, a
oil of gladness on our heads, A place than all be-
friend holds fellowship with friend Though sunder'd far, by
sin and sense molest no more; And heav'n comes down our

sure re - treat: 'Tis found beneath the mer - cy - seat.
-sides more sweet, It is the blood-bought mer - cy - seat.
faith they meet, Around one common mer - cy - seat.
souls to greet, While glory crowns the mer - cy - seat.

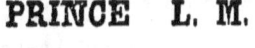

PRINCE L. M.   A. J. C.

1. Great God, indulge my humble claim; Be thou my
2. Thou great and good, thou just and wise, Thou art my
3. With heart and eyes, and lift-ed hands, For thee I
4. I'll lift my hands, I'll raise my voice, While I have

hope, my joy, my rest; The glo-ries that compose thy
Fa-ther and my God; And I am thine by sa   cred
long, to thee I look; As trav-el-lers in thirst-y
breath to pray or praise: This work shall make my heart re -

name   Stand all engaged to make me blest.
ties,— Thy. son, thy ser - vant bought with blood.
lands   Pant for the cool - ing wa - ter - brook.
-joice, And fill the rem - nant of my days.

HUMILITY. L. M.

Altered and Arranged from RINK.

1. Wherefore should man, frail child of clay, Who,
2. His bright-est vis-ions just ap-pear, Then
3. Fol-lies and crimes, a count-less sum, Are
4. God of my life! Fa-ther di-vine! Give

from the cradle to the shroud, Lives but the in-sect
van-ish, and no more are found: The stateliest pile his
crowd-ed in life's lit-tle span: How ill, a-las, does
me a meek and low-ly mind; In mod-est worth, O

of a day,— O why should mor-tal man be proud?
pride can rear, A breath may lev-el with the ground
pride become That erring, guil-ty crea-ture, man!
let me shine, And peace in hum-ble vir-tue find.

JURA. L. M.*   SWISS.

1. Thus saith the high and lof - ty One 'I
2. But I descend to worlds be - low; On
3. The humble soul my words re - vive: I
4. O may thy pard'ning grace be nigh, Lest

sit up - on my ho - ly throne; My name is God; I
earth I have a man - sion too; The hum - ble spir - it
bid the mourning sin - ner live; Heal all the broken
we should faint, despair, and die! Thus shall our bet - ter

dwell on high; Dwell in my own e - ter - ni - ty.
and contrite Is an a - bode of my de - light.
hearts I find, And ease the sor - rows of the mind.
thc'ts approve The methods of thy chast'ning love

* From "Mendelssohn Collection," by Permission.

[7*]

STONEFIELD. L. M.

1. God is our ref - uge and defence; In trouble
2. Yea, though the earth's foundation rock, And mountains
3. There is a river pure and bright, Whose streams make
4. Built by the word of his command, With his un

our un - fail - ing aid; Se - cure in his om
down the gulf he hurl'd, His peo - ple smile a -
glad the heavenly plains; Where in e ter - ni -
cloud - ed pres - ence blest, Firm as his throne the

nip o - tence What foe can make our souls a - fraid.
mid the shock: They look beyond this transient world.
- ty of light The cit - y of our God remains.
bulwarks stand; There is our home, our hope, our rest.

DEVON. C. M. ARRANGED. 79

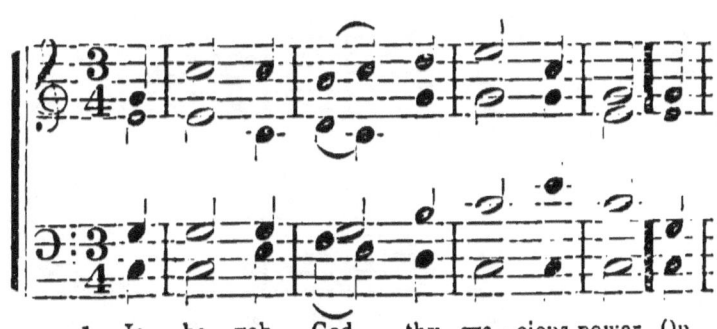

1. Je-ho-vah, God, thy gra-cious power, On
2. If on the wings of morn we speed, To
3. Thy power is in the o-cean deeps, And
4. From morn till noon— till la-test eve, Thy

eve-ry hand we see; O may the bless-ings
earth's re-mot-est bound, Thy hand will there our
reach-es to the skies; Thine eye of mer-cy
hand, O God, we see; And all the bless-ings

of each hour Lead all our thoughts to thee.
journey lead, Thine arm our path sur-round.
nev-er sleeps, Thy goodness nev-er dies.
we re-ceive, Pro-ceed a-lone from thee.

HEBER. C. M.

G. KINGSLEY.

1. Fa - ther of spir - its, na - ture's God, Our
2. Could we, on morning's swiftest wings, Fly
3. In vain may guilt at - tempt to fly, Con -
4. Search thou our hearts, and there de - stroy Each

tho'ts are known to thee; Thou, Lord, canst hear each
thro' the track - less air, Or dive beneath deep
ceal'd by dark - est night; One glance from thy all -
se - cret bo - som sin, And fit us for those

i - dle word, And ev' - ry ac - tion see.
o - cean's springs, Thy presence would be there.
piercing eye Can bring it all to light.
realms of joy, That we may en - ter in.

FRANKLIN. C. M.

S. B. POND.
By permission.

1. Plunged in a gulf .... of dark de-spair, We wretched
2. With pitying eyes .... the Prince of peace Beheld our
3. Down from the shin - ing seats a - bove, With joyful
4. O for this love.... let rocks and hills Their lasting

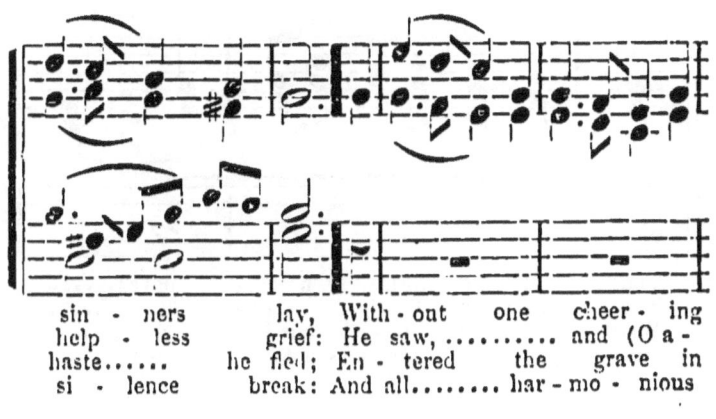

sin - ners lay, With-out one cheer-ing
help - less grief: He saw, ... and (O a-
haste...... he fled; En - tered the grave in
si - lence break: And all........ har - mo - nious

beam of hope, Or spark.... of glimm'ring day.
- maz ing love!) He flew.... to our re - lief.
mor tal flesh, And dwelt a - mong the dead.
hu - man tongues, The Sa - viour's prais - es speak.

PIETY. C. M.
T. CLARK.

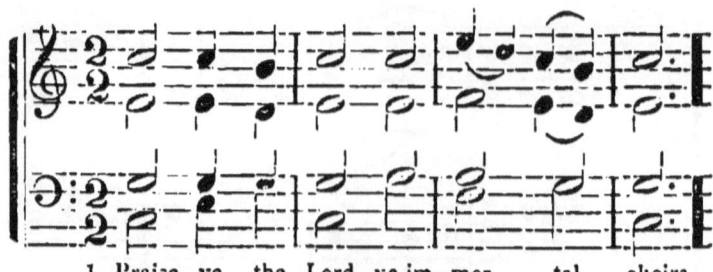

1. Praise ye the Lord, ye im-mor-tal choirs
2. Shine to his praise, ye crys--tal skies,
3. Thou rest-less globe, of gol--den light,
4. Shout to the Lord, ye surg-ing seas,

That fill the worlds a--bove;......
The floor of his a--bode;......
Whose beams cre-ate our days,......
In your e-ter--nal roar;......

That fill the worlds a---bove,
The floor of his a---bode;
Whose beams cre-ate our days,
In your e-ter--nal roar.

HOWARD. C. M.
MRS. CUTHBERT.

1. O God we praise thee, and con-fess, That
2. To thee all an-gels cry a-loud, To
3. O ho-ly, ho-ly, ho-ly Lord, Whom
4. The apostle's glorious com-pa-ny, And

thou the on-ly Lord, And ev-er-last-ing
thee the powers on high, Both cher-u-bim and
heavenly hosts o-bey, The world is with the
prophets, crown'd with light, With all the mar-tyrs'

Fath-er art, By all on earth a-dor'd.
ser-a-phim, Con-tin-ual--ly do cry,—
glo-ry fill'd, Of thy ma-jes-tic sway.
no-ble host, Thy con-stant praise re-cite.

FLORENCE. C. M. GERMAN.

By permission.

1. O happy man, whose soul is fill'd With
2. A careful providence will stand, And
3. Thy wife shall be a fruitful vine; Thy
4. The Lord will thy best hopes fulfil, For

zeal and rev'rend awe! His lips to God their
ever guard thy head: Will on the labors
children round thy board, Each like a plant of
months and years to come; The Lord, who dwells on

honors yield, His life adorns the law.
of thy hand Its kindly blessings shed.
honor shine, And learn to fear the Lord.
Zion's hill, Will send the blessings home.

[8]

HAPPINESS. C. M.

Subject from RINK.

1. My soul, how love - ly is the place, To
2. There the great monarch of the skies His
3. With his rich gifts the heaven - ly Dove De -
4. There, mighty God, thy works de - clare Tho

which thy God re - sorts! 'Tis heaven to see his
saving pow'r dis - plays; And light breaks in up -
scends, and fills the place; While Christ reveals his
se - crets of thy will; And still we seek thy

smil - ing face, Tho' in his earth - ly courts.
on our eyes, With kind and quick - ning rays.
won - drous love, And sheds a - broad his grace.
mer - cies there; And sing thy prais - es still.

SHEPHERD. C. M.   ENGLISH AIR.   87

1 When ris-ing from the bed of death, O'er-
2. If yet while par-don may be found, And
3. When thou, O Lord, shalt stand dis-closed In
4. O may my bro-ken, con-trite heart, Time-

whelmed with guilt and fear, I view my Ma-ker
mer-cy may be sought, My soul with in-ward
maj-es-ty severe. And sit in judgment
-ly my sins lament; And ear-ly, with re

face .... to face, O how shall I ap-pear.
hor - ror shrinks, And trembles at the thought.
on .... my soul,— O how shall I ap-pear?
pent - ant tears, E-ter-nal wo pre-vent.

BETHLEHEM. C. M.

Arranged from Leach.

1. As shepherds watch'd their flocks by night, All seat-ed on the ground, The an-gel of the Lord came down, And glo-ry shone around.
2. Fear not, said he, (for migh-ty dread Had seized their troub-led mind,) Glad ti-dings of great joy I bring, To you and all mankind.
3. To you, in Da-vid's town, this day Is born of Da-vid's line, The Sa-viour, who is Christ the Lord; And this shall be the sign:
4. The heavenly babe you there shall find To hu-man view displayed, All mean-ly wrapp'd in swath-ing bands, And in a man-ger laid.

LANESBORO. C. M.

1. Sov'reign of all the worlds on high, Allow my humble
2. My Father, God! that gracious word Dispels my guil-ty
3. Come, Holy Ghost, thyself impress On my ex-pand-ing
4. Cheer'd by that witness from on high Unwav'ring I be-

claim; Nor while, unwor-thy, I draw nigh, Nor while, un-
fear; Not all the notes by an-gels heard, Not all the
heart: And show that in the Fath-er's grace, And show that
lieve: And Ab-ba, Fath-er, hum-bly cry; And Ab-ba,

wor-thy I draw nigh, Disdain a Father's name.
notes by an-gels heard, Could so de-light my ear.
in the Fath-er's grace, I share a fil-ial part.
Father hum-bly cry; Nor can the sign de-ceive.

[8*]

HANOVER. C. M.

1. And must I be to judgment brought, And
2. Yes eve-ry se-cret of my heart Shall
3. How care-ful then ought I to live; With
4. Thou aw-ful judge of quick and dead, The

an - swer in that day For eve-ry vain and
short - ly be made known, And I re-ceive my
what re - lig - ious fear: Who such a strict ac-
watch - ful power be-stow; So shall I to my

i - dle thought, And eve - ry word I say!
just de - sert For all that I have done.
count must give For my be - ha - viour here.
ways take heed, To all I speak or do.

ORTONVILLE. C. M. II. 91

From the Mendelssohn Coll., by permission.

1. Fa - ther of Jesus Christ, my Lord, My Saviour and my
2. Thou know'st for my offence he died, And rose again for
3. E - ter - nal life to all mankind Thou hast in Jesus
4. Faith, mighty faith the promise sees, And looks to that a

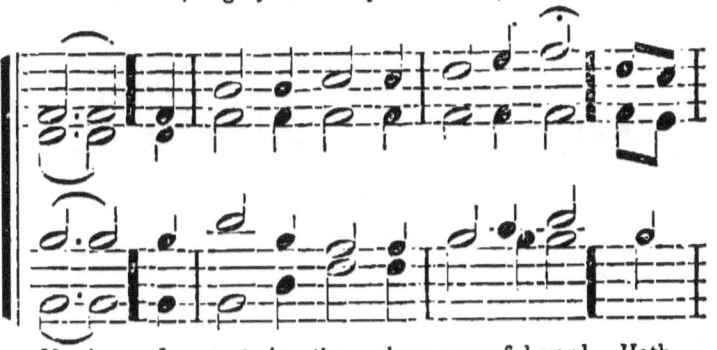

Head, I trust in thee, whose powerful word Hath
me, Ful - ly and free - ly jus - ti - fied, That
given; And all who seek, in him shall find The
lone, Laughs at im - pos - si - bil - i - ties, And

raised him from the dead, Hath raised him from the dead,
I might live to thee, That I might live to thee.
hap - piness of heaven, The happi - ness of heaven.
cries 'It shall be done!' And cries 'It shall be done!'

CONWAY. C. M. ENGLISH.

1. Before thy mercy seat, O Lord, Behold, thy servants
2. Let thy e-ter-nal truths, we pray, Dwell richly in each
3. Lord, from thy word remove the seal, Unfold its hid-den
4. Help us to see the Saviour's love Beaming from eve-ry

stand, To ask the knowl-edge of thy word, To
heart: That from the safe and nar-row way That
store: And as we hear, O may we feel And
page; And let the thoughts of joy above And

ask the knowledge of thy word, The guidance of thy hand.
from the safe and narrow way We nev-er may de-part.
as we hear, O may we feel Its val-ue more and more.
let the tho'ts of joy a-bove, Our in-most souls engage.

DEVIZES. C. M.   TUCKER.   93

1. Je-sus, with all thy saints above, My tongue would
2. Bless'd be the Lamb, my dearest Lord, Who bought me
3. The Lamb that freed my captive soul From Satan's
4. All glo-ry to the dy-ing Lamb, And nev-er

bear her part; Would sound a-loud thy sav-ing love,
with his blood; And quench'd his Father's flam-ing sword,
hea-vy chains; And sent the li-on down to howl,
ceasing praise! While an-gels live, to know his name

And sing thy bleeding heart, And sing thy bleeding heart.
In his own vi-tal flood, In his own vi-tal flood.
Where hell and horror reigns, Where hell and hor-ror reigns.
Or saints to feel his grace, Or saints to feel his grace.

SHEPHAM. C. M.   DR. DUPUIS.

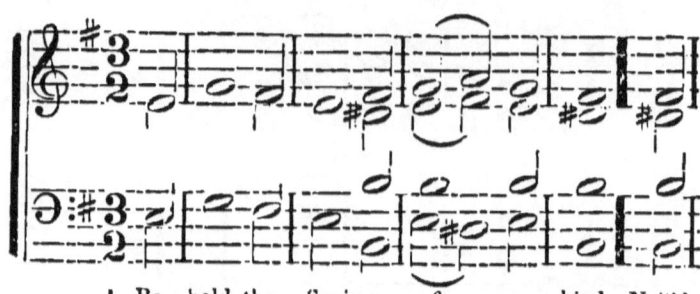

1. Be-hold the Saviour of man-kind Nail'd
2. Hark! how he groans, while na-ture shakes, And
3. 'Tis done! the precious ran-som's paid! Re-
4. But soon he'll break death's en-vious chain, And

to the shame-ful tree; How vast the love that
earth's strong pil-lars bend; The tem-ple's veil in
ceive my soul! he cries; See where he bows his
in full glo-ry shine; O Lamb of God, was

him in-clined To bleed and die for thee!
sun- -der breaks; The sol- id mar-bles rend.
sa- -cred head; He bows his head, and dies.
ev- -er pain, Was ev- -er love like thine?

WOODLAND. C. M. GOULD. 95

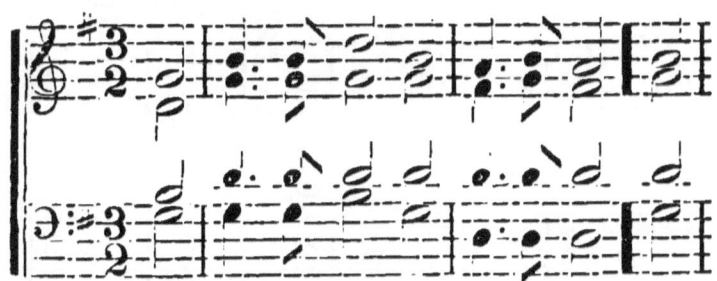

1. Mis-tak-en souls! that dream of heaven, And
2. Vain are our fan-cies, ai-ry flights, If
3. 'Tis faith that chan-ges all the heart, 'Tis
4. 'Tis faith that con-quers earth and hell, By

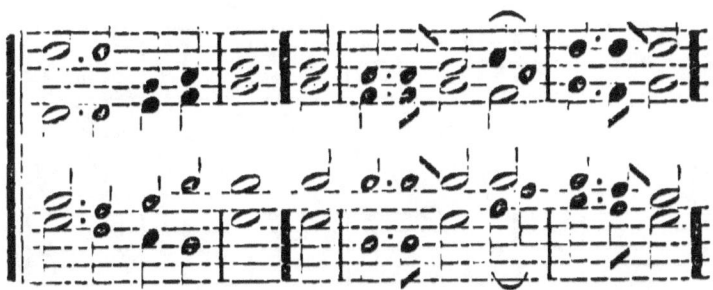

make their empty boast Of inward joys and sins forgiven,
faith be cold and dead; None but a liv-ing power unites,
faith that works by love, That bids all sin-ful joys de-part,
a ce-les-tial power; This is the grace that shall prevail,

Of inward joys and sins forgiven, While they are slaves to lust.
None but a liv-ing power u-nites, To Christ the living Head.
That bids all sin-ful joys depart, And lifts the tho'ts above.
This is the grace that shall prevail, In the de-ci-sive hour.

DELIGHT. C. M.

By permission.

1. Thy cease-less, un-ex-hausted love, Un-mer-i-
2. Thou wait-est to be gracious still; Thou dost with
3. Thy good-ness and thy truth to me. To eve-ry
4. Its streams the whole cre-a-tion reach, So plenteous

Tutti.

ted and free, Un-mer-i-ted and free, Delights our
sin-ners bear; Thou dost with sin-ners bear; That, saved, we
soul, a-bound; To eve-ry soul, a-bound; A vast, un-
is the store; So plen-teous is the store; E-nough for

e-vil to re-move, And help our mis-e-ry.
may thy good-ness feel, And all thy grace de-clare.
fath-om-a-ble sea, Where all our thoughts are drown'd.
all, e-nough for each, Enough for-ev-er-more.

ARLINGTON. C. M. — DR. ARNE. 97

1. Fa-ther, how wide thy glo-ry shines! How
2. Those mighty orbs pro-claim thy power; Their
3. But when we view thy strange de-sign, To
4. Here the whole De-i-ty is known, Nor

high thy won-ders rise! Known thro' the earth by
mo-tions speak thy skill; And on the wings of
save re-bel-lious worms, Where vengeance and com-
dares a crea-ture guess, Which of the glo-ries

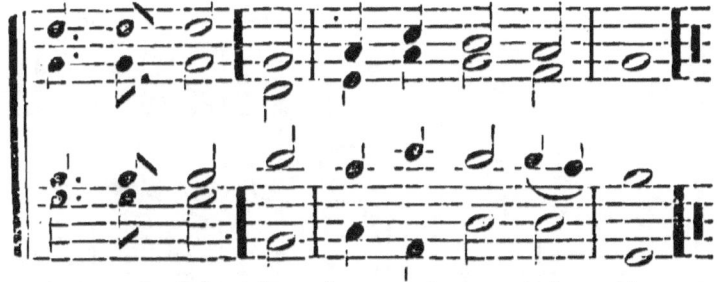

thou-sand signs, By thou-sands through the skies.
eve-ry hour, We read thy pa-tience still.
pas-sion join, In their di-vin-est forms.
bright-est shone, The jus-tice, or the grace

[9]

DODDRIDGE. C. M.

Altered from GOULD.

1. A - las! and did my Sa - viour bleed? And
2. Was it for crimes that I have done, He
3. Well might the sun in dark - ness hide, And
4. Thus might I hide my blush - ing face, While

did my Sove - reign die? Would he de - vote that
groan'd up - on the tree? A - maz - ing pi - ty!
shut his glo - ries in, When Christ, the migh - ty
his dear cross ap - pears: Dis - solve my heart in

sa - cred head, For such a worm as I?
grace un - known! And love be - yond de - gree!
Ma - ker dies, For man, the crea - ture's sin,
thank - ful - ness, And melt mine eyes to tears.

STONEVILLE. C. M.

By permission.

1. Faith is the bright-est ev-i-dence Of
2. It sets time past in pres-ent view, Brings
3. By faith we know the world was made By
4. Ab-ra'm o-beyed the Lord's command, From

things be-yond our sight; It pier-ces through the
dis-tant pros-pects home, Of things a thou-sand
God's al-migh-ty word; We know the heavens and
his own coun-try driven; By faith he sought a

veil of sense, And dwells in heav-enly light.
years a-go, Or thou-sand years to come.
earth shall fade, And be a-gain re-stored.
promised land, But found his rest in heaven.

100 BRATTLE STREET. C. M. DOUBLE.
PLEYEL.

1. O for a thou-sand tongues to sing, My
2. Je-sus! the name that charms our fears, That
3. He speaks, and list'ning to his voice, New

great Redeem-er's praise; The glories of my
bids our sor-rows cease; 'Tis mu-sic in the
life the dead re-ceive; The mournful broken

God and King, The tri-umphs of his grace.
sin-ner's ears, 'Tis life, and health, and peace.
hearts re-joice; The hum-ble poor be-lieve.

My gra-cious Mas - ter, and my God, As-
He breaks the power of can-cell'd sin, He
Hear him, ye deaf; his praise, ye dumb, Your

sist me to pro - claim,— To spread thro' all the
sets the pris' - ner free; His blood can make the
loos-ened tongues em - ploy; Ye blind, behold your

earth abroad. The hon - ors of thy Name.
foul - est clean; His blood a - vail'd for me.
Sa-viour come; And leap, ye lame, for joy.

[9*]

DEDHAM. C. M.
WM. GARDNER.

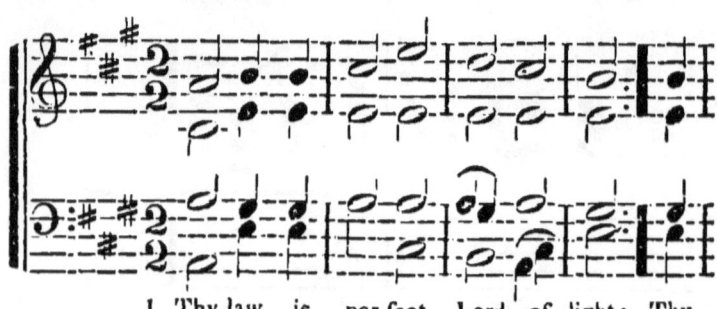

1. Thy law is per-fect, Lord of light; Thy
2. Let these, O God, my soul con-vert, And
3. By these may I be warned be-times; Who
4. So may the words my lips ex-press,—The

tes - ti - mo - nies sure; The stat-utes of thy
make thy ser - vant wise; Let these be glad-ness
knows the guile with-in? Lord, save me from pre-
thoughts that throng my mind; O Lord, my strength and

realm are right, And thy com-mandments pure.
to my ears— The day-spring to mine eyes.
sump-tuous crimes; Cleanse me from se-cret sin.
righ-teous-ness, With thee ac-cept-ance find

UNITY. C. M. ARRANGED FROM READ.

1. Lo, what an en-ter-tain-ing sight,
2. When streams of love, from Christ the spring,
3. 'Tis like the oil, di-vine-ly sweet,
4. 'Tis pleasant as the morn-ing dews,

Are brethren who a - gree! Brethren, whose
De - scend to ev' - ry soul, And heavenly
On Aaron's rev' - rend head: The trickling
That fall on Zi - on's hill; Where God his

cheerful hearts unite In bands of pi - e - ty!
peace, with balmy wing. Shades and be - dews the whole.
drops perfum'd his feet, And o'er his gar - ments spread.
mildest glo - ry shews, And makes his grace dis - til.

ALBERT. C. M.
CROFT.

1. Thus I resolv'd be-fore the Lord, 'Now will I
2. If I am e'er constrain'd to stay With men of
3. I'll scarce allow my lips to speak The pi-ous
4. Yet if some prop-er hour ap-pear, I'll not be

watch my tongue, Lest I let slip one sin-ful word,
lives pro-fane, I'll set a double guard that day,
tho'ts I feel; Lest scoffers should th' oc-ca-sion take
o ver-awed; But let the scoffing sin-ners hear,

Or do my neighbor wrong.' Or do my neigh-bor wrong.
Nor let my talk be vain, Nor let my talk be vain.
To mock my ho-ly zeal, To mock my ho-ly zeal.
That I can speak for God, That I can speak for God.

IDDO. C. M.

Arranged from NAGELI.

1. I want a principle within, Of jealous, godly fear; A sen-si-bil-i-ty of sin,— A pain to feel it near, A pain to feel it near.
2. Quick as the apple of an eye, O God, my conscience make; A-wake my soul when sin is nigh, And keep it still a-wake, And keep it still a-wake.
3. If to the right or left I stray, That moment, Lord, re-prove; And let me weep my life a-way, For having grieved thy love, For having grieved thy love.
4. O may the least omission pain My well-in-structed soul, And drive me to the blood a-gain, Which makes the wounded whole, Which makes the wounded whole.

EPHESUS. C. M.
C. MEINECKE.
By permission.

1. Father to thee my soul I lift; My soul on thee de-
2. Mercy and grace are thine alone, And pow'r and wisdom
3. We cannot speak one useful word, One holy tho't con-
4. His blood demands the purchased grace, His blood's availing

Instrument.

-pends: Convinced that every perfect gift From thee alone de-
too: Without the Spirit of thy Son, We nothing good can
ceive, Unless, in answer to our Lord, Thyself the blessing
plea Obtained the help for all our race: And sends it down to

scends, Convinc'd that ev'ry perfect gift, From thee alone descends.
do, Without the Spirit of thy Son, We nothing good can do.
give, Unless, in answer to our Lord, Thyself the blessing give.
me, Obtained the help for all our race: And sends it down to me.

PILGRIM. C. M. ARRANGED. 107

1. Hap-py the child whose ten-der years Re-
2. 'Twill save us from a thousand snares To
3. To thee, Al-migh-ty God, to thee Our
4. Let the sweet work of prayer and praise Em-

ceive in-struction well; Who hates the sin-ner's
seek re-lig-ion young; Grace will preserve our
childhood we re-sign; 'Twill please us to look
ploy our youngest breath; Thus we're prepared for

path, and fears The road that leads to hell.
foll'wing years, And make our vir-tue strong.
back and see That our whole lives were thine.
long-er days, Or fit for ear-ly death.

JEWELL. C. M. ARR. FROM LUTHER.

1. Let eve-ry tongue thy good-ness speak, Thou
2. When sorrows bow the spir-it down, When
3. Thou know'st the pains thy ser-vants feel, Thou
4. Thy mer-cy nev-er shall re-move From

sov'reign Lord of all; Thy strength'ning hands up-
vir-tue lies distress'd, Be neath the proud op-
hear'st thy children's cry; And their best wish-es
men of heart sin-cere: Thou sav'st the souls whose

-hold the weak, And raise the poor that fall.
-pressor's frown, Thou giv'st the mourn-er rest.
to ful-fil, Thy grace is ev-er nigh.
hum-ble love Is join'd with ho-ly fear.

HAMMOND. C. M. — GOULD. 109

1. How sad our state by nature is; Our
2. But there's a voice of sov'reign grace Sounds
3. My soul obeys the gracious call, And
4. To the blest fountain of thy blood, In-

sin how deep it stains; And Satan binds our
from the sacred word: Ho! ye despairing
runs to its relief; I would believe thy
-carnate God I fly; Here let me wash my

captive souls Fast in his slavish chains.
sinners come, And trust a faithful Lord.
promise Lord; O help my unbelief.
guilty soul From crimes of deepest dye.

[10]

COLLISTER. C. M.

ENGLISH AIR.
By permission.

1. From whence these direful o - mens round, Which
2. Well may the earth, as - ton - ish'd shake, And
3. Be - hold, fast - streaming from the tree, His
4. For me these pangs his soul as - sail; For

heaven and earth a - maze? And why do earthquakes
na - ture sym - pathize,— The sun, as dark - est
all - a - ton - ing blood: Is this the In - fi -
me this death is borne; My sins gave sharpness

cleave the ground? Why hides the sun his rays?
night be black; Their Maker, Jesus, dies?
- nite? 'tis he,— My Saviour and my God.
to the nail, And pointed every thorn.

FEAR. C. M. By permission.

1. Ter - ri - ble tho't! shall I a - lone, Who
2. While all my old com pan - ions dear, With
3. Shall I, amidst a ghast - ly band, Dragg'd
4. Ah! no;— I still may turn and live, For

may be saved, shall I, Of all a-
whom I once did live, Joy - ful at
to the judg - ment - seat, Far on the
still his wrath de - lays; He now vouch

- las! whom I have known, Thro' sin for - ev - er die?
God's right hand ap - pear, A bless - ing to receive.
left with hor - ror stand, My fear - ful doom to meet?
safes a kind re - prieve, And of - fers me his grace.

112. WAUGH. C. M. R. A. SMITH.

1. This is the day the Lord hath made; O
2. The Stone the builders set at nought, That
3. Christ is that Stone, re-ject-ed once, And
4. This is the day the Lord hath made; O

earth, re-joice and sing: Let songs of tri-umph
Stone has now be-come The sure foun-da-tion,
number'd with the slain; Now raised in glo-ry,
earth, re-joice and sing: With songs of tri-umph

hail the morn; Ho-san - na to our King!
and the strength Of Zi - on's heavenly dome.
o'er his Church E-ter - nal-ly to reign.
hail the morn; Ho-san - na to our King!

BALERMA. C. M.

1. O hap-py is the man who hears Re-
2. For she has treasures great-er far Than
3. Her right hand of-fers to the just, Im-
4. And as her ho-ly la-bors rise, So

li-gion's warn-ing voice, And who ce-les-tial
east or west un-fold; More pre-cious are her
mor-tal, hap-py days; Her left im-per-ish-
her re-wards in-crease: Her ways are ways of

wis-dom makes, His ear-ly, on-ly choice.
bright re-wards, Than gems or stores of gold.
a-ble wealth, And heav-enly crowns dis-plays.
pleas ant-ness, And all her paths are peace.

[10*]

JERUSALEM. C. M. DOUBLE.

E. L. WHITE.

1. How did my heart re-joice to hear, My
2. Peace be with-in this sa-cred place, And

friends de-vout-ly say, 'In Zi-on let us
joy a con-stant guest! With ho-ly gifts and

all ap-pear, And keep the sol-emn day!'
heav-enly grace, Be her at-tend-ants blest.

115

I love her gates, I love the road! The
My soul shall pray for Zi - on still While

church, adorn'd with grace, Stands like a pal - ace
life or breath re - mains; Here my best friends, my

built for God, To show his mild - er face.
kindred dwell, Here God, my Saviour reigns.

FOUNTAIN. C. M.

A. J. C.

1. There is a foun-tain fill'd with blood, Drawn
2. The dying thief re-joiced to see That
3. Thou dying Lamb! thy precious blood Shall
4. E'er since, by faith I saw the stream Thy

from Imman-uel's veins; And sinners, plunged be
fountain in his day; And there may I, though
never lose its power, Till all the ransom'd
flowing wounds sup-ply, Re-deeming love has

neath that flood, Lose all their guil-ty stains.
vile as he, Wash all my sins a-way.
Church of God Are saved, to sin no more.
been my theme, And shall be till I die.

GILLETT. C. M.

Arranged from a Mss. of E. C. STOCKTON.

1. Hark, the glad sound! the Saviour comes, The
2. He comes, the Pris'ner to release, In
3. He comes, the broken heart to bind, The
4. Our glad hosannas, Prince of peace, Thy

Saviour promised long; Let every heart pre
Satan's bondage held; The gates of brass be
wounded soul to cure, And with the treasures
welcome shall proclaim, And heaven's eternal

-pare a throne, And every voice a song.
-fore him burst, The iron fetters yield.
of his grace, T'enrich the humble poor.
arches ring With thy beloved name.

WARWICK. C. M. STANLEY.

1. That dole - ful night be - fore his death, The
2. To keep the feast, Lord, we have met, And
3. Thy suff'- rings, Lord, each sa - cred sigh To
4. O tune our tongues, and set in frame Each

Lamb for sin - ners slain, Did, al - most with his
to re - mem - ber thee: Help each poor trembler
our re - membrance brings: We eat the bread, and
heart that pants for thee, To sing— Ho - san-na

dy - ing breath, This sol - emn feast proclaim.
to re - peat, For me he died, for me!
drink the wine, But think on nobler things.
to the Lamb, The Lamb that died for me!

PERPETUITY. C. M. ENGLISH.

1. O God, our help in a-ges past, Our hope for years to
2. A thousand ages, in thy sight, Are like an evening
3. Time, like an ever-rolling stream, Bears all its sons a-
4. The busy tribes of flesh and blood, With all their cares and

come, Our shelter from the stormy blast, And our e-
gone; Short as the watch that ends the night, Be - fore the
- way; They fly, forgotten, as a dream Dies at the
fears, Are carried downward by the flood, And lost in

ter - nal home, And our e - ter - nal home.
ris - ing sun, Be - fore the ris - ing sun.
op' - ning day, Dies at the op' - ning day.
foll' - wing years, And lost in foll' - wing years

COVINGTON. C. M. D.

GRARDINI.

1. Come, Ho-ly spir-it, heaven-ly Dove, With
2. Fa-ther, and shall we ev-er live At

all thy quick'ning powers: Kin-dle a flame of
this poor dy-ing rate; Our love so faint, so

sa-cred love In these cold hearts of ours;
cold to thee, And thine to us so great;

Look how we grov-el here be-low, Fond
Come, Ho ly Spir-it, heaven-ly Dove, With

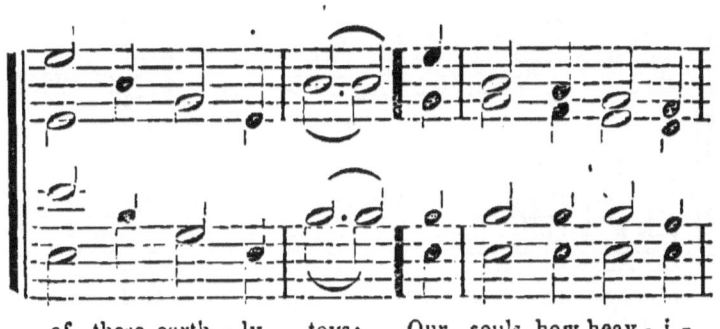

of these earth-ly toys; Our souls, how heav-i-
all thy quick'ning powers; Come, shed abroad a

-ly they go, To reach e-ter nal joys.
Sa-viour's love, And that shall kin-dle ours.
[11]

122 EGREMONT. C. M. EARL OF WILTON.
By permission.

1. O that the Lord would guide my ways, To
2. O send thy Spir - it down— to write Thy
3. From van-i ty turn off my eyes; Let
4. Or - der my foot - steps by thy word, And

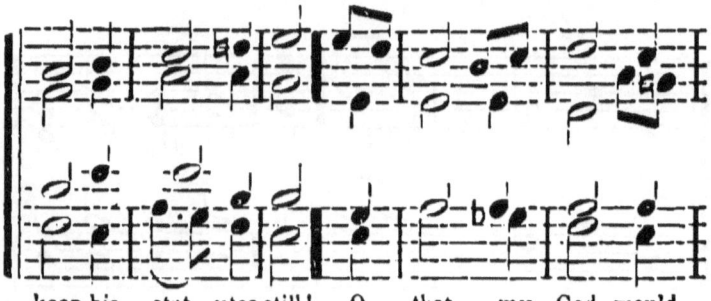

keep his stat - utes still! O that my God would
law up - on my heart! Nor let my tongue in -
no cor - rupt design, Nor cov - et - ous de -
make my heart sincere: Let sin have no do -

grant me grace, To know and do his will.
- dulge de - ceit, Nor act the li - ar's part.
- sires, a - rise With-in this soul of mine.
min ion, Lord; But keep my con - science clear.

GERMANY. C. M. GERMAN CHORAL. 123

1. Lord, I esteem thy judgments right, And
2. Thy precepts of-ten I sur- vey; I
3. My heart, in midnight si-lence cries, 'How
4. And when my spir-it drinks her fill, At

all thy stat-utes just; Thence I main-tain a
keep thy law in sight, Thro' all the busi-ness
sweet thy com-forts be!' My thoughts in ho-ly
some good word of thine, Not migh-ty men, that

con-stant fight With eve-ry flatt'-ring lust.
of the day, To form my ac-tions right.
won-der rise, And bring their thanks to thee.
share the spoil, Have joys compared to mine.

TALLIS. C. M.

TALLIS.

1. O Char-i-ty, thou heavenly grace! All tender,
2. The man of char-i-ty ex-tends To all his
3. 'Tis love that makes relig-ion sweet; 'Tis love that
4. Then let us all in love a-bound, And char-i-

soft and kind! A friend to all the
lib'-ral hand; His kin-dred, neigh-bors,
makes us rise With will-ing minds and
-ty pur-sue; Thus shall we be with

hu-man race, To all that's good in-clin'd.
foes and friends His pi-ty may com-mand.
ar-dent feet, To yonder hap-py skies.
glo-ry crown'd, And love as an-gels do.

ZERAH. C. M. ARRANGED.

1. To us a child of hope is born, To
2. His name shall be the Prince of peace, For-
3. His power in-creas-ing, still shall spread; His
4. To us a child of hope is born, To

us a Son is given; Him shall the tribes of
-ev - er more a-dored; The Wonder - ful, the
reign no end shall know: Jus-tice shall guard his
us a Son is given; The Won-der - ful, the

earth o - bey, Him, all the hosts of heaven.
Coun - sel - lor, The great and mighty Lord.
throne a - bove, And peace a - bound be - low.
Coun - sel - lor, The migh - ty Lord of heaven.

[11*]

BOLTON. C. M.   ENGLISH.

1. O Lord, my best de-sire ful-fil, And
2. Why should I shrink at thy command, Whose
3. No, let me rath-er free-ly yield What
4. Wis-dom and mer-cy guide my way, Shall

help me to re-sign Life, health, and com-fort
love for-bids my fears? Or tremble at thy
most I prize, to thee Who nev-er hast a
I re-sist them both? A poor blind crea-ture

to thy will, And make thy pleas - ure mine.
gracious hand, That wipes a - way my tears?
good with-held, Or wilt with-hold from me.
of a day? And crush'd be-fore the moth!

DOWNS. C. M. GERMAN.

From the DULCIMER.

1. Prayer is the soul's sin-cere desire, Ut-
2. Prayer is the bur-den of a sigh,—The
3. Prayer is the simplest form of speech The
4. Prayer is the Christian's vi-tal breath, The

ter'd or un-ex-pressed; The mo-tion of a
fall-ing of a tear,— The upward glanc-ing
in-fant lips can try: Prayer, the sub-li-mest
Christian's na-tive air. His watchword at the

hid-den fire That trembles in the breast.
of an eye, When none but God is near.
strains that reach The Maj-es-ty on high.
gates of death, He en-ters heaven with prayer.

MARLOW. C. M. GREGORIAN.

1. O for a heart to praise my God, A
2. A heart re-sign'd, sub-missive, Meek, My
3. O for a lowly, con-trite heart, Be-
4. A heart in eve-ry thought renewed, And

heart from sin set free;— A heart that al-ways
great Re-deem-er's throne; Where on-ly Christ is
liev-ing, true and clean; Which nei-ther life nor
full of love di-vine; Per-fect, and right, and

feels thy blood So free-ly spilt for me.
heard to speak, Where Je-sus reigns a-lone.
death can part From him that dwells with-in.
pure and good, A cop-y, Lord, of thine.

LITCHFIELD. C. M. VENITIAN MELODY.

1. Ye hearts with youthful vigor warm, In smil-ing crowds draw near; And turn from ev'-ry mor-tal charm, A Sa-viour's voice to hear.
2. He, Lord of all the worlds on high, Stoops to con-verse with you; And lays his radiant glo-ries by, Your wel-fare to pur-sue.
3. What ob-ject, Lord my soul should move, If once compared to thee? What beau-ty should com-mand my love, Like what in Christ I see.
4. A way, ye false, de-lusive toys, Vain tempt-ers of the mind! 'Tis here I fix my last-ing choice, And here true bliss I find.

IRISH. C. M.   A. J. C.

1. With joy we med-i-tate the grace Of
2. Touch'd with a sym-pa-thy with-in, He
3. He, in the days of fee-ble flesh, Pour'd
4. He'll nev-er quench the smoking flax, But

our High Priest a bove; His heart is made of
knows our fee - ble frame: He knows what sore temp
out strong cries and tears, And in his meas - ure
raise it to a flame; The bruis - ed reed he

ten - der - ness, His bowels melt with love.
- ta - tions mean, For he hath felt the same.
feels a - fresh What every mem - ber bears.
nev - er breaks, Nor scorns the mean - est name.

NAOMI. C. M.

Arranged from REED.

1. Lord, all I am is known to thee; In
2. Thy all-sur-round-ing sight sur-veys My
3. My tho'ts lie o-pen to thee, Lord, Be-
4. O wondrous knowledge! deep and high: Where

vain my soul would try To shun thy pres-ence,
ris-ing and my rest, My pub-lic walks, my
-fore they're form'd within, And ere my lips pro-
can a crea-ture hide? Within thy circ-ling

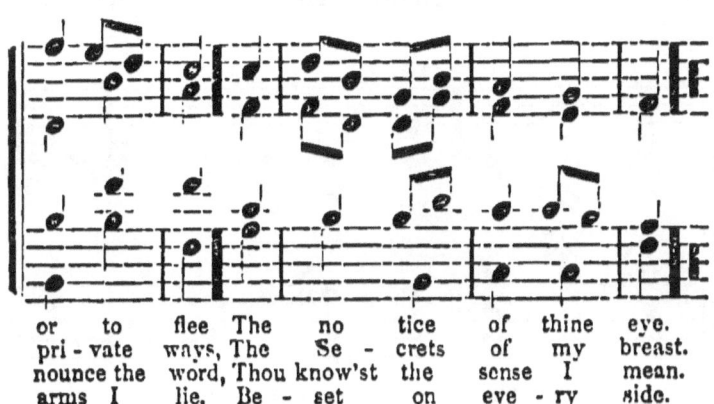

or to flee The no-tice of thine eye.
pri-vate ways, The Se-crets of my breast.
nounce the word, Thou know'st the sense I mean.
arms I lie, Be-set on eve-ry side.

VARINA. C. M. D.

G. F. ROOT.
By permission.

1. There is a land of pure de-light, Where
2. Sweet fields be-yond the swelling flood Stand

saints im - mor - tal reign; In - fi - nite day ex-
dressed in liv - ing green; So to the Jews old

- cludes the night, And pleasures ban - ish pain;
Ca - naan stood, While Jor - dan rolled be - tween;

There ev-er-last-ing spring a-bides, And
Could we but climb where Mo-ses stood, And

nev-er-with'-ring flow'rs; Death, like a nar-row
view the landscape o'er, Not Jordan's stream nor

sea, di-vides This heavenly land from ours.
death's cold flood, Should fright us from the shore.

[12]

HEINER. C. M.
J H. HEWITT.

1. Great God! how in-finite art thou, What worthless
2. Thy throne e - ter - nal ages stood, Ere seas or
3. E - ter - ni - ty, with all its years, Stands present
4. Our lives thro' varying scenes are drawn, And vexed with

worms are we; Let the whole race of crea - tures
stars were made: Thou art the ev - er liv - ing
in thy view; To thee there's nothing old ap -
tri - fling cares, While thine e - ter - nal thought moves

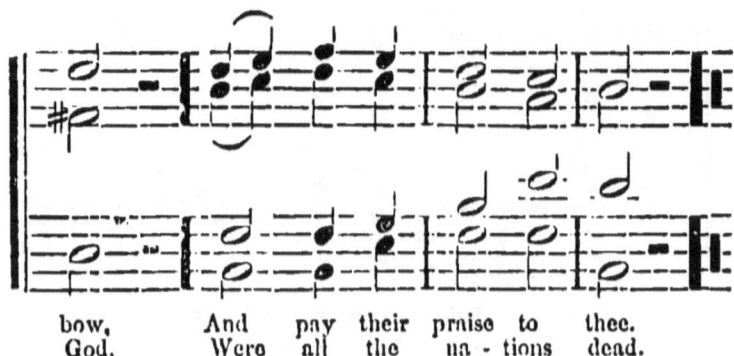

bow, And pay their praise to thee.
God, Were all the na - tions dead.
- pears; Great God! there's noth - ing new.
on Thine un - dis turbed af fairs.

SILVER STREET. S. M. — SMITH. 135

1. Come sound his praise a-broad, And hymns of
2. He form'd the deeps un-known; He gave the
3. Come, worship at his throne, Come, bow be-
4. To-day at-tend his voice, Nor dare pro

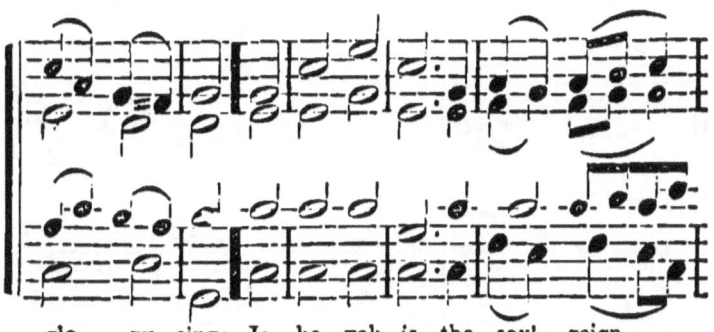

glo- ry sing; Je-ho-vah is the sov'-reign......
seas their bound; The wat'ry worlds are still his......
fore the Lord; We are his works, and not our......
voke his rod; Come, like the people of his......

God, The u - - ni-ver - sal King.
own, And all.......... the sol - id ground.
own, He form'd...... us by his word.
choice, And own........ your gra - cious God.

136   CRANBROOK. S. M.   SMITH.

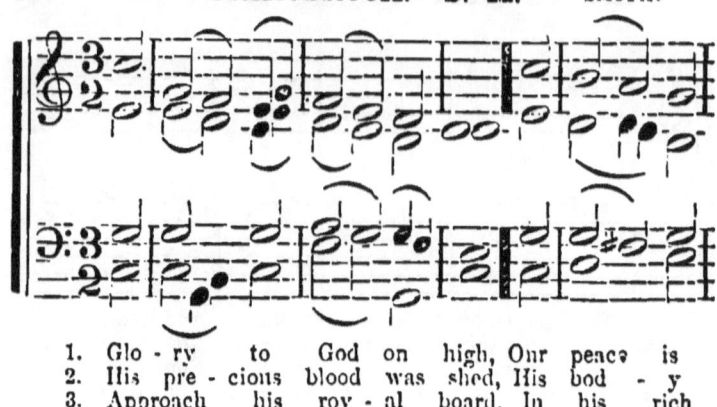

1. Glo - ry to God on high, Our peace is
2. His pre - cious blood was shed, His bod - y
3. Approach his roy - al board, In his rich
4. The Fa - ther gives the Son; The Son his

made...... with Heaven; The Son of God came
bruised.... for sin: Re - mem - ber this in
gar - - ments clad; Join ev' - ry tongue to
flesh........ and blood: The Spir - it seals; and

down to die, That we .... might be forgiven.
eat - ing bread, And this in drink - ing wine.
praise the Lord, And eve - ry heart be glad.
faith puts on The right - cous - ness of God.

138 LANSDALE. S. M. D. CORRELLI.

1. The thing my God doth hate, That
2. That bless-ed law of thine, Je-

I no more may do, Thy creature, Lord a-
-sus, to me im-part; The Spirit's law of

-gain cre-ate, And all my soul re-new:
life di-vine, Oh write it on my heart!

1. What cheering words are these! Their sweetness
2. 'Tis well when joys a-rise, 'Tis well when
3. 'Tis well when at his throne They wrestle,
4. 'Tis well when Jesus calls, From earth and

who can tell? In time and to e-ter-ni-
sorrows flow; 'Tis well when darkness veils the
weep, and pray; 'Tis well when at his feet they
sin, A-rise, Join with the hosts of vir-gin

-ty, 'Tis with the right-eous well.
skies, And strong temp-ta-tions blow.
groan, Yet bring their wants a-way
souls, Made to sal-va-tion wise.

LATHROP. S. M.   WESTERN AIR.   141

1. Not all the blood of beasts, On Jew-ish
2. But Christ the heavenly Lamb Takes all our
3. My faith would lay her hand On that dear
4. My soul looks back to see The bur-dens

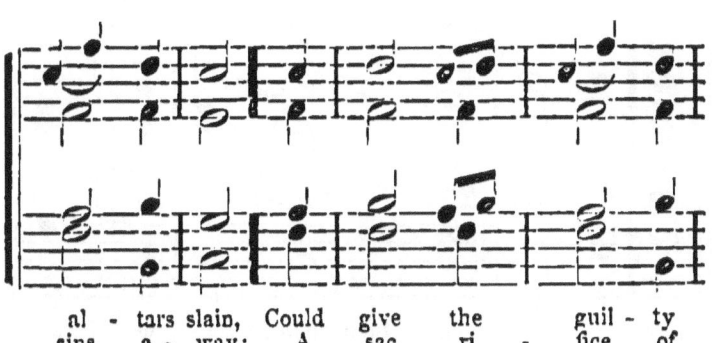

al - tars slain, Could give the guil - ty
sins a - way; A sac - ri - fice of
head of thine,— While like a pen - i -
thou didst bear,— When hang - ing on the

con - science peace, Or wash a - way the stain.
no - bler name, And rich - er blood than they.
tent I stand, And there con - fess my sin.
curs - ed tree,— And hopes her guilt was there.

BALLSTON. S. M.

By permission.

1. The man is ev-er blest Who shuns the sinner's ways: A-mongst their coun-cils nev-er stands, Nor takes the scorn-er's place.
2. But makes the law of God His study and de-light, A-midst the la-bors of the day And watch-es of the night.
3. He like a tree shall thrive With waters near the root; Fresh as the leaf his name shall live, His works are heaven-ly fruit.
4. Not so th' un-god-ly race, They no such blessing find; Their hopes shall flee like emp-ty chaff Be-fore the driv-ing wind.

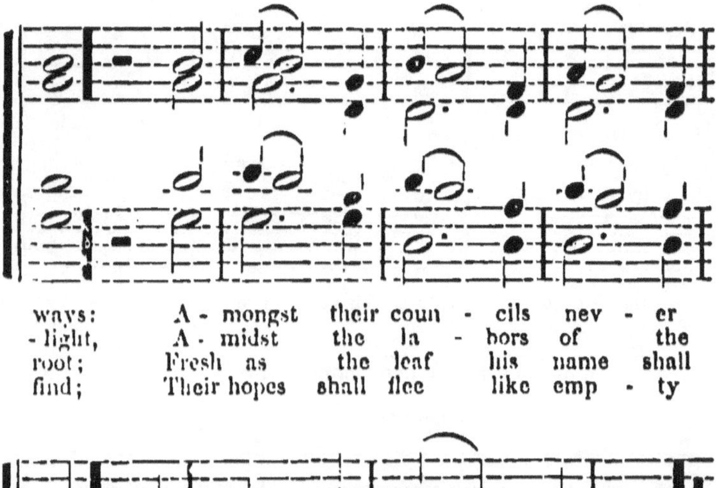

BACKUS. S. M. A. J. C. 143

1. In ex pec - ta - tion sweet, We
2. He comes! the Conqu'ror comes; Death
3. The trumpet sounds,— A - wake!— Ye
4. Thrice hap - py morn for those Who

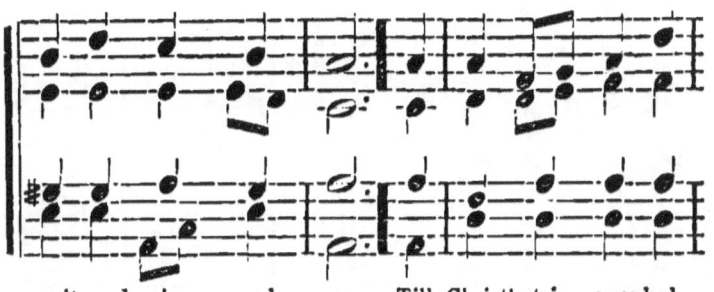

wait, and sing and pray, Till Christ's tri - umphal
falls be - neath his sword; The joy - ful pris'ners
dead, to judg - ment come! The pil - lars of cre-
love the ways of peace: No night of sor - row

car we meet, And see an end - less day.
burst their tombs, And rise to meet their Lord.
a - tion shake, While hell re - ceives her doom.
e'er shall close, Or shade their per - fect bliss.

MARCUS. S. M. A. J. C.

1. The Lord my Shepherd is, I shall be well sup-plied;
2. He leads me to the place Where heav'nly pasture grows;
3. If e'er I go a-stray, He doth my soul re-claim;

Cres - - cen - do.

Since he is mine and I am his, What can I want be-side?
Where living wa-ters gently pass, And full salvation flows,
And guides me in his own right way For his most holy name;

Since he is mine and I am his, What can I want be-side?
Where living waters gently pass, And full salvation flows.
And guides me in his own right way, For his most holy name.

DOOMSDAY. S. M.   ENGLISH.   145

1. Behold! with aw-ful pomp The Judge prepares to
2. Nature in wild a-maze, Her dis-so-lu-tion
3. The liv-ing look with dread; The frighted dead a-
4. Horrors all hearts appal; They quake, they shriek, they

come; Th' arch-an-gel sounds the dreadful trump, And
mourns: Blush-es of blood the moon de-face, The
rise, Start from the mon-u-ment-al bed, And
cry; Bid rocks and mountains on them fall; But

wakes the gen'-ral doom, And wakes the gen'-ral doom.
sun to darkness turns, The sun to darkness turns.
lift their ghastly eyes, And lift their ghastly eyes
rocks and mountains fly, But rocks and mountains fly.

[13]

MURDOCH. S. M. A. J. C.

1. There is be-yond the sky; A heaven of
2. There is a dreadful hell, And ev-er-
3. Can such a child as I Es-cape this
4. Then will I read and pray, While I have

joy and love, And ho-ly children, when they
-last-ing pains; There sinners must with dev-ils
aw-ful end? And may I hope, when-e'er I
life and breath; Lest I should be cut off to-

die, Go to that world a-bove.
dwell, In dark-ness, fire, and chains.
die, I shall to heav'n as-cend.
day, And sent t' e-ter-nal death.

THATCHER. S. M. — HANDEL. 147

1. Je - sus, thou source di - vine, Whence
2. None else will heaven ap - prove: Thou
3. Here let our feet a - bide, Nor
4. Safe through this world of night, Lead

hope and comfort flow, Je - sus, no oth - er
art the on - ly way, Or - dain'd by ev - er
from thy path de - part; Di - rect our steps, thou
to the blissful plains, The re - gions of un -

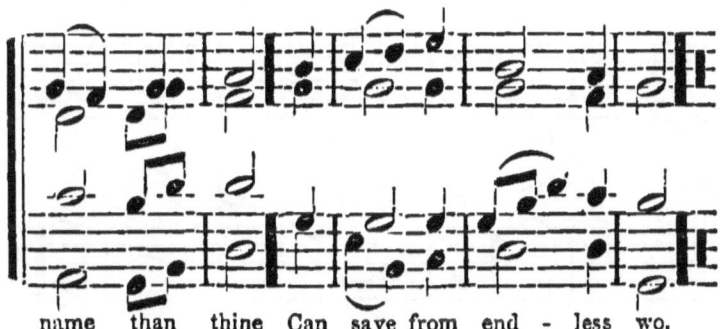

name than thine Can save from end - less wo.
- last - ing love, To realms of end - less day.
gra - cious Guide! And cheer the faint - ing heart.
cloud - ed light, Where joy for ev - er reigns.

ST. THOMAS. S. M.
A. WILLIAMS.

1. What maj-es-ty and grace, Through
2. Down from his throne on high, The
3. The debt that sin-ners owed, Up-
4. There our High Priest ap-pears, Be-

all the gos-pel shine! 'Tis God that speaks, and
mighty Sa-viour comes; Lays his bright robes of
-on the cross he pays; Then through the clouds as-
-fore his Fa-ther's throne; Min-gles his mer-its

we con-fess The doc-trine most di-vine.
glo-ry by, And fee-ble flesh as-sumes.
cends to God, 'Midst shouts of lof-tiest praise.
with our tears, And pours sal-va-tion down.

TELEMAN. S. M. 149

1. The Lord is risen indeed; The grave has
2. The Lord is risen in - deed; He lives to
3. The Lord is risen in deed; At-tend-ing
4. Then take your gold-en lyres, And strike each

lost its prey; With him shall rise the ran-som'd
die no more; He lives, his peo-ple's cause to
an-gels hear; Up to the courts of heaven, with
cheerful chord: Join, all ye bright ce-les-tial

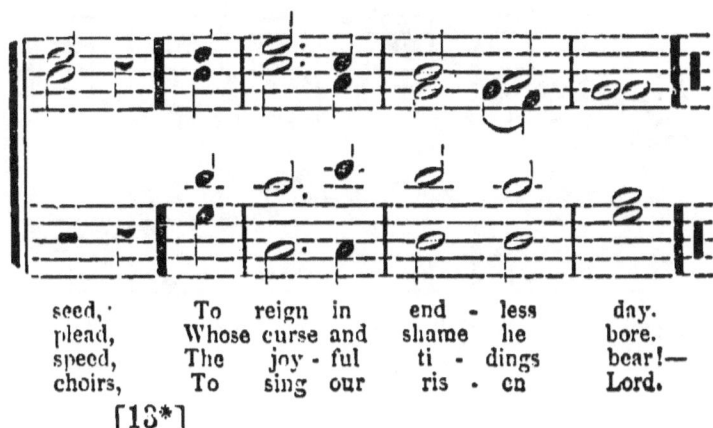

seed, To reign in end-less day.
plead, Whose curse and shame he bore.
speed, The joy-ful ti-dings bear!—
choirs, To sing our ris-en Lord.

[13*]

150 PAINSVILLE. S. M. D. HADAWAY.

1. The praying spir-it breathe, The
2. Swift to my res-cue come, Thy

watching power im-part; From all en-tan-gle-
own this mo-ment seize; Gath-er thy wand'ring

-ments beneath Call off my peaceful heart:
spir-it home, And keep in per-fect peace;

151

My fee-ble mind sus-tain, By
Suf-fered no more to rove O'er

world-ly tho'ts op-prest, Ap-pear and bid me
all the earth a-broad, Ar-rest the pris'-ner

turn a-gain To my e-ter-nal rest.
of thy love, And shut me up in God.

HOFFMAN. S. M.

A. J. C

1. Our sins on Christ were laid; He bore the mighty load: Our ran-som-price he ful-ly paid In groans and tears and blood.
2. To save a world he dies; Sin-ners be-hold the Lamb! To him lift up your long-ing eyes; Seek mer-cy in his name.
3. Par-don and peace a-bound; He will your sins forgive; Sal-va-tion in his name is found, He bids the sin-ner live.
4. Je-sus, we look to thee:— Where else can sin-ners go? Thy bound-less love shall set us free From wretched-ness and wo.

DESIRE. S. M.

From an American Tune.

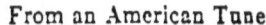

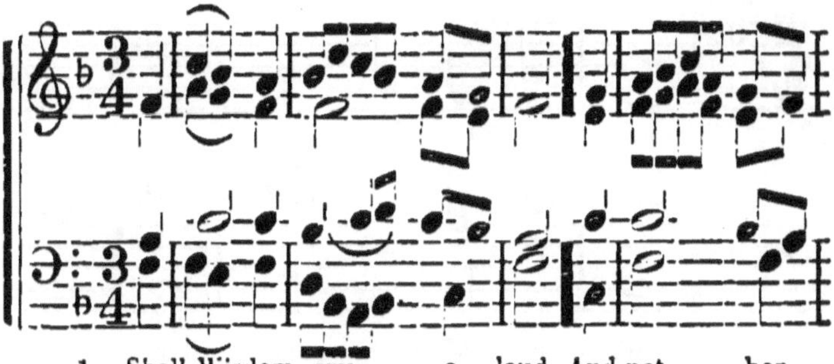

1. Shall Wisdom cry a - loud, And not her
2. 'I was his chief de - light, His ev - er -
3. My bus - y thoughts at first, On their sal -
4. Then come, receive my grace, Ye chil - dren,

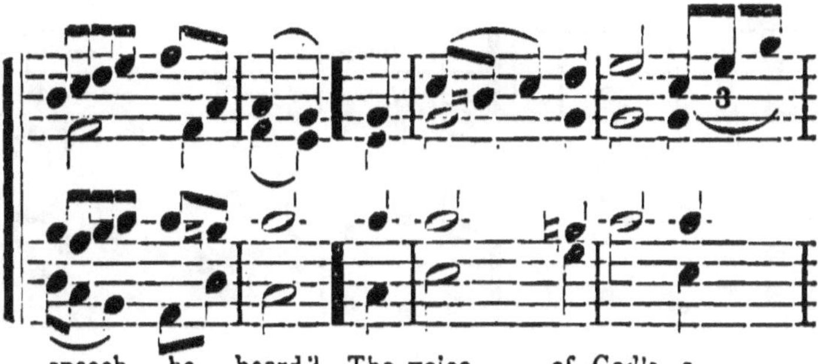

speech be heard? The voice of God's e
- last - ing Son, Be - fore the first of
va - tion ran, Ere sin was born, or
and be wise; Hap - py the man who

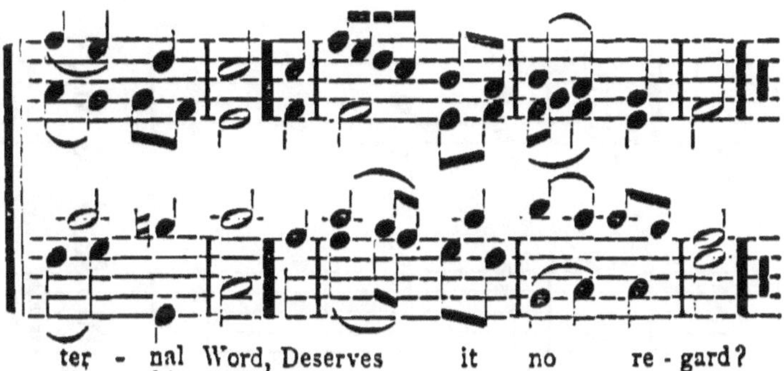

ter - nal Word, Deserves it no re - gard?
all his works, Cre - a - tion, was be - gun.
Ad - am's dust Was fash - ion'd to a man.
keeps my ways; The man, who shuns them, dies.'

154. PALERMO. S. M. ANCIENT TUNE.

1. Spir-it of faith, come down, Re-
2. 'Tis thine the blood t' ap - ply, And
3. No man can tru - ly say That
4. O that the world might know The

veal the things of God; And make to us the God-head
give us eyes to see, That he who did for sin - ners
Je - sus is the Lord, Un - less thou take the veil a-
all - a - ton - ing Lamb! Spir-it of faith de - scend and

known, And wit - ness with the blood.
die, Hath sure - ly died for me.
- way, And breathe the liv - ing word.
show The vir - tue of his name.

LISBON. S. M. READ. 155

1. Wel-come, sweet day of rest, That
2. The King him-self comes near, And
3. One day in such a place, Where
4. My will-ing soul would stay In

saw the Lord a-rise; Wel-come to this re-
feasts his saints to-day; Here we may sit, and
thou my God, art seen, Is sweet-er than ten
such a frame as this, And sit and sing her-

-viv-ing breast, And these re-joic-ing eyes!
see him here, And love, and praise, and pray.
thousand days Of pleas-ur-a-ble sin.
self a-way To ev-er-last-ing bliss.

156 DOVER. S. M. ENGLISH AIR.

1. My son, know thou the Lord; Thy
2. Call, while he may be found; Seek
3. If thou wilt seek his face, His
4. But if thou leave thy God, Nor

fa-ther's God o bey; Seek his pro-tect-ing
him while he is near; Serve him with all thy
ear will hear thy cry; Then shalt thou find his
choose the path to heaven; Then shalt thou per-ish

care by night, His guardian hand by day.
heart and mind, And wor-ship him with fear.
mer-cy sure, His grace for-ev-er nigh.
in thy sins, And nev-er be for-given.

HENSHAW. S. M.
DR. WM. BOYCE.

1. Fa-ther, our hearts we lift Up to thy
2. His in-fant cries pro-claim A peace 'twixt
3. The gift unspeak-a-ble We thankful-
4. May all mankind re-ceive The new-born

gra-cious throne, And thank thee for the
earth and heaven: Sal-va-tion, through his
-ly re-ceive, And to the world thy
Prince of peace, And meek-ly in his

precious gift Of thine In-car-nate Son.
on-ly Name, To all man-kind is given.
goodness tell, And to thy glo-ry live.
spir-it live, And in his love in-crease.

WATCHMAN. S M. — LEACH.

LANE. S. M. — HERRING.

1. Lord, how shall sinners dare Look
2. Bright terrors guard thy seat, And
3. My soul, with cheerful eye See
4. Teach my weak heart, O Lord, With

up to thine abode? Or offer their im-
glories veil thy face; Yet mercy calls us
where thy Saviour stands,— The glorious Ad-vo-
faith to call thee mine; Bid me pronounce the

-perfect prayer, Before a holy God?
to thy feet, And to thy throne of grace.
-cate on high, With incense in his hands.
blissful word—Father—with joy divine.

LABAN. S. M. SCOTCH AIR. 161

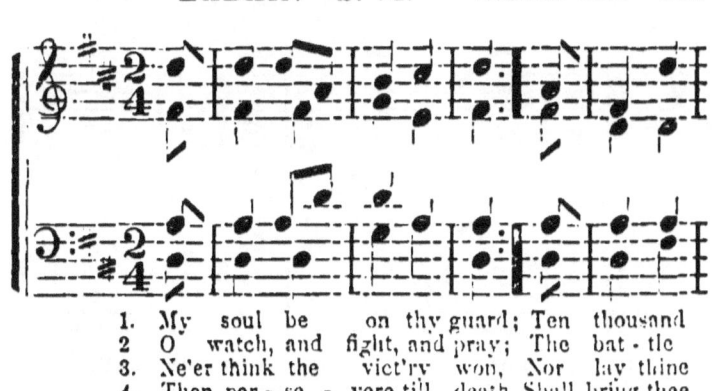

1. My soul be on thy guard; Ten thousand foes arise: The hosts of sin are pressing hard, To draw thee from the skies.
2. O watch, and fight, and pray; The battle ne'er give o'er; Renew it boldly every day, And help divine implore.
3. Ne'er think the vict'ry won, Nor lay thine armor down: The work of faith will not be done, 'Till thou obtain the crown.
4. Then persevere till death Shall bring thee to thy God; He'll take thee, at thy parting breath, To his divine abode.

[14*]

SLICER. S. M.
J. W. ALBY.

1. My few re-volv-ing years, How swift they
2. A dark and cloud-y day, Made up of
3. Lord, thro' a-noth-er year, If thou per-

glide a-way! How short the term of life ap-
grief and sin; A host of dang'rous foes with-
mit my stay, With watch-ful care will I pur-

pears, When past, 'tis but a day!
out, And guilt and fear with in.
sue, The true and liv-ing way!

MORRIS. S. M.   W. A. TARBUTTON.   163

1. O where shall rest be found! Rest for the
2. The world can nev-er give The bliss for
3. Beyond this vale of tears, There is a

wea - ry soul? 'Twere vain the o - cean's depths to
which we sigh; 'Tis not the whole of life to
life a - bove, Un-measured by the flight of

sound, Or pierce to eith - er pole.
live, Nor all of death to die.
years— And all that life is love.

165

Be - fore the throne, &c.
His blood a - tones, &c.
For - give him, O, &c.
With con - fi - dence, &c.

Be - fore the throne my Sure - ty stands, My
His blood a - tones for all our race, And
For - give him, O for - give, they cry, Nor
With con - fi - dence I now draw nigh, And

fore the throne, &c. Before the throne, &c.
blood atones, &c. His blood atones, &c.
give him, O, &c. For - give him, O, &c.
confidence, &c. With con - fi - dence, &c.

name is writ - ten on his hands, My name is
sprinkles now the throne of grace, And sprink - - les
let that ransom'd sin - ner die, Nor let that
Fa - ther, Ab - ba, Father, cry, And Fa - - ther,

writ - - - ten on his hands.
now the throne of grace.
ran - - - som'd sin - ner die.
Ab - ba, Fa - ther, cry.

166. ASHTON. L. M. 6 lines, or 11. 8.

GERMAN AIR. By permission.

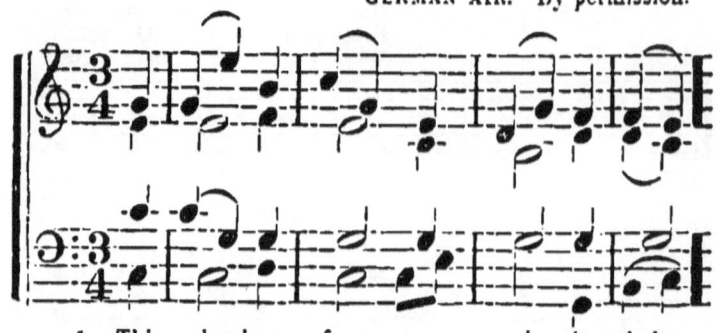

1. This slumber from my spir-it shake;
2. O wouldst thou, Lord, thy ser-vant guard
3. O nev-er suf-fer me to sleep,
4. At-tend-ed by that sa-cred dread,

Warn'd by the Spir-it's in - - - ward call,
'Gainst eve-ry known or se - - cret foe;
Se-cure with-in the verge of hell;
And wise from e-vil to de-part,

Let me to right-eous-ness a-wake,
A mind for all as-saults pre-pared,
But still my watch-ful spir-it keep
Let me from strength to strength pro-ceed,

NASHVILLE. L. P. M. or H. 2.

A. J. CLEAVELAND.

1. Fa - ther of Je - sus Christ, the Just,
2. If drawn by thy al - lur - ing grace,
3. The gift un - speak - a - ble im - part,

My Friend and Ad - vo - cate with thee,
My want of liv - ing faith I feel,
Com - mand the light of faith to shine,

Pit - y a soul that fain would trust
Show me in Christ thy smil - ing face,
To shine in my dark, droop - ing heart,

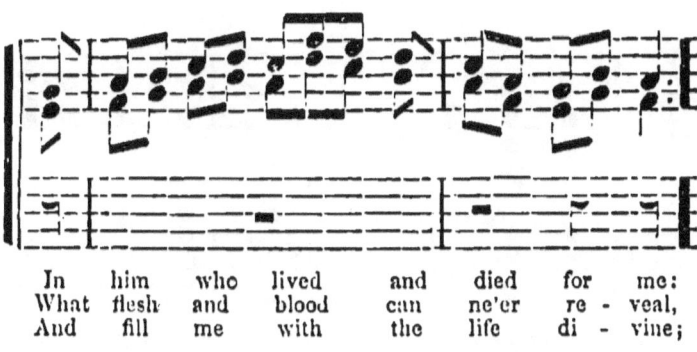

In him who lived and died for me:
What flesh and blood can ne'er re-veal,
And fill me with the life di-vine;

But on-ly thou canst make him known,
Thine all-re-deem-ing Son dis-play,
Now bid the new cre-a-tion be,

And in my heart re-veal thy Son.
And call my darkness in to day.
C God, let there be faith in me!

[15]

170 NEWCOURT. L. P. M. or H. 2. H. BOND.

1. I'll praise my Maker with my breath;
2. How blest the man whose hopes rely,

And when my voice is lost in death,
On Is-rael's God, he made the sky,

Praise shall em-ploy my no-bler powers.
And earth and seas with all their train,

My days of praise shall ne'er be past,
His truth for-ev er stands se-cure;

While life and thought, and be - ing last,
He saves th' oppressed, he feeds the poor,

Or im - mor - tal - i ty en dures.
And none shall find his pres ence vain.

LIGHTNER. L. M.
J. TABLER.

1. From all that dwell be-low the skies, Let
2. E-ter-nal are thy mer-cies, Lord, And

the Cre-a-tor's praise a-rise; Je-hovah's glorious name be
truth e-ter-nal is thy word; Thy praise shall sound from shore to

sung, Through eve-ry land, by eve-ry tongue.
shore, 'Till suns shall rise and set no more.

LITTLE. 8 & 7s, or III. 3.

1. Ho-ly Spirit! Fount of blessing, Ev-er
2. Seal of truth, and bond of u-nion, Source of
3. Heavenly Guide from paths of er-ror, Comfort-
4. Promised Pledge! Eter-nal Spir-it! Greater

watchful ev - er kind; Thy ce - les - tial aid pos -
light, and flame of love, Symbol of di - vine com -
er of minds distressed, When the bil - lows fill with
than all gifts be - low, May our hearts thy grace in -

sessing, Pris - on'd souls de - liv' - rance find.
munion, In the ol - ive - bear - ing dove.
terror, Point ing to the ark of rest.
herit: May our lips thy glo - ries show.

[15*]

175

To thine a-bode my heart as-pires: With warm de-
They praise thee still; and hap-py they Who love the
Oh glorious seat; when God our King Shall thith-er

sires to see my God. To thine a-bode my heart as
way to Zi-on's hill: They praise thee still; and hap-py
bring our willing feet. Oh glorious seat; when God our

pires; With warm de- sires to see my God.
they, Who love the way to Zi-on's hill.
King Shall thith-er bring our will-ing feet!

176 SOLITUDE. H. M. or II. I. ARRANGED.

1. Sin - ners, lift up your hearts,
2. Je - sus is glo - ri - fied,
3. To make an end of sin,
4. From heaven he shall once more

The prom - ise to re - ceive;
And gives the Com - fort - er,
And Sa - tan's work de - stroy,
Tri - umph - ant - ly de - scend,

Je - sus him - self im - parts,—
His Spir - it, to re - side
He brings his king - dom in,—
And all his saints re - store

178 ARNON. C. P. M. or II. I.

1. Thou God of power, thou God of love,
2. Thee as our God we too would claim,
3. The veil that hides thy glo-ry rend,

Whose glo-ry fills the realms a-bove,
And bless the Sa-viour's prec-ious Name,
And here in sav-ing power de-scend.

Whose praise arch-an-gels sing,
Through whom this grace is given;
And fix thy blest a-bode;

And veil their faces while they cry,
He bore the curse to sinners due,
Here to our hearts thyself reveal,

Thrice Holy, to their God Most High,
He forms their ruined souls anew,
And let each waiting spirit feel

Thrice Holy, to their King.
And makes them heirs of heaven.
The presence of our God.

180 MOZART. 8s & 7s Double. or III. 3.

MOZART.

1. One there is a - bove all others, Well deserves the
2. When he lived on earth a - based, Friend of sinners

name of friend; His is love be - yond a brother's,
was his name; Now a - bove all glo - ry rais - ed,

Cost - ly, free, and knows no end; Which of all our
He re - joic - es in the same; O, for grace our

friends to save us, Could or would have shed his blood?
hearts to soften, Teach us, Lord, at length to love;

But this Sa - viour died to have us
We, a las! for - get too of - ten,

Re - con - ciled in him to God.
What a friend we have a - bove.

[16*]

182 SMYRNA. 8s & 7s Double. or III. 3.

ARRANGED.

1. { Je-sus, I my cross have taken, All to
   { Naked, poor, de-spised, for-saken, Thou from
2. { Soul, then know thy full sal-va-tion, Rise, o'er
   { Joy to find in eve-ry station Something

Yet how rich is my con-dition! God and
Think that Je-sus died to win thee; Child of

End.

leave and fol-low thee;
hence, my all shall be;   Per-ish eve-ry
sin, and fear, and care,
still to do or bear;   Think what spir it

heaven are still my own.
heaven, canst thou re-pine?

D. C.

fond am-bi-tion, All I've sought, or hoped, or known
dwells with-in thee, Think what Father's smiles are thine;

HAPPY LAND. P. M.

1. There is a happy land, far, far away, Where saints in
2. Come to this happy land, come, come away; Why will ye
2. Bright in that happy land, beams every eye; Kept by a

glory stand, Bright, bright as day; O how they sweetly sing,—
doubting stand? Why still de-lay? O we shall happy be,
Father's hand, Love cannot die; O, then, to glo-ry run;

Worthy is our Savior King; Loud let his praises ring forever more.
When, from sin and sorrow free, Lord, we shall live with thee, blest
[evermore.
Be a crown and kingdom won, And, bright above the sun, reign
[evermore

184. SNOWFIELD. 7s. or III. I. From HAYDN.

Or 8s & 7, by omitting the slurs at the end of the first and third lines.

1. Hark! the herald an - gels sing,— Glory to the
2. Joyful all ye na - tions rise— Join the triumphs
3. Christ, by highest heaven a - dored, Christ, the ever -
4. Hail the heav'n-born Prince of peace, Hail the Son of

new-born King; Peace on earth and mer - cy mild;
of the skies; With an - gel - ic hosts pro - claim,—
last - ing Lord; Veil'd in flesh the God - head see;
righteous - ness! Light and life to all he brings,—

God and sin - ners rec - on - ciled.
Christ is born in Beth - le - hem.
Hail, in - car - nate De - i - ty!
Risen with heal - ing in his wings.

OTTO. 7s, or III. I.   A. J. CLEAVELAND.

1. Sinners, turn, while God is near; Dare not
2. Cries, Ye will not hap-py be; No, ye
3. Turn, he cries, ye sin-ners, turn: By his
4. If your death were his de-light, Would he

think him in - sin-cere: Now, e'en now, your Saviour
will not come to me,— Me who life to none de-
life, your God hath sworn; He would have you turn and
you to life in - vite? Would he ask, be-seech and

stands; All day long he spreads his hands.
-ny; Why will ye re-solve to die?
live; He would all the world re-ceive.
cry,— Why will ye re-solve to die?

[16*]

186 HEATH. 7s Double. or III. I. From ROSINI.

1. Saviour, when in dust to thee, Low we
2. By thy birth and ear - ly years, By thy
3. By thine hour of dark de - spair, By thine

bow th' a-dor-ing knee; When, re - pent - ant, to the
human griefs and fears, By thy fast - ing and dis -
ag - o - ny of prayer, By the pur - ple robe of

skies Scarce we lift our streaming eyes;
tress In the lone - ly wil - der - ness;
scorn, By thy wounds, thy crown of thorn,

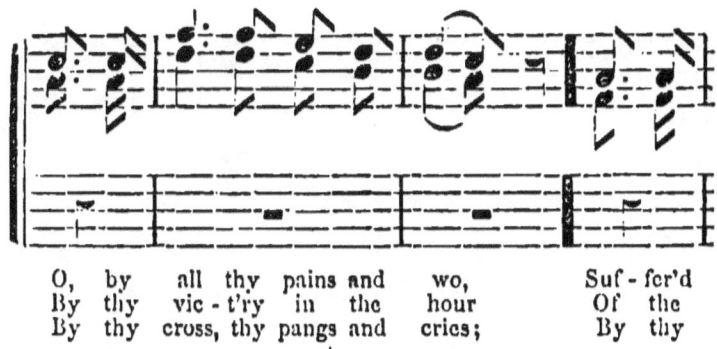

O, by all thy pains and wo, Suf-fer'd
By thy vic-t'ry in the hour Of the
By thy cross, thy pangs and cries; By thy

once for man be - low, Bending from thy throne on
subtle Tempter's power; Je - sus, look with pitying
perfect sac - ri - fice; Je - sus, look with pitying

high, Hear our sol - emn lit - a - ny.
eye: Hear our sol - emn lit - a - ny.
eye: Hear our sol - emn lit - a - ny.

HOTHAM. 7s. III. 1. MOORE.

1. Sinners, turn; why will ye die? God, your
2. He the fa-tal cause de-mands; Asks the
3. Sinners, turn; why will ye die? God, your
4. Will ye let him die in vain? Cru-ci-

Ma-ker, asks you why? God, who did your be — ing
work of his own hands, Why, ye thankless crea — tures
Sa-viour, asks you why, He, who did your souls re-
fy your Lord a-gain! Why, ye ransom'd sin — ners,

give, Made you for him-self to live.
why Will ye cross his love and die?
trieve, Died him-self, that ye might live.
why Will ye slight his grace, and die?

ROCK OF AGES. 7s 6 lines. or III. 2.

1. Rock of a ges! cleft for me, Let me
2. Should my tears for - ev - er flow, Should my
3. While I draw this fleeting breath, When mine

Be of sin the double cure, Save from
In my hand no price I bring, Sim - ply
Rock of a - ges! cleft for me, Let me

hide my - self in thee, Let the wa - ter and the
zeal no languor know, This for sin could not a -
eye - lids close in death, When I rise to worlds un -

wrath, and make me pure.
to thy cross I cling.
hide my - self in thee.

blood, From thy side a heal - ing flood,
tone, Thou must save, and thou a - lone;
known, And be - hold thee on thy throne;

SPRING. 7s or III. 1.

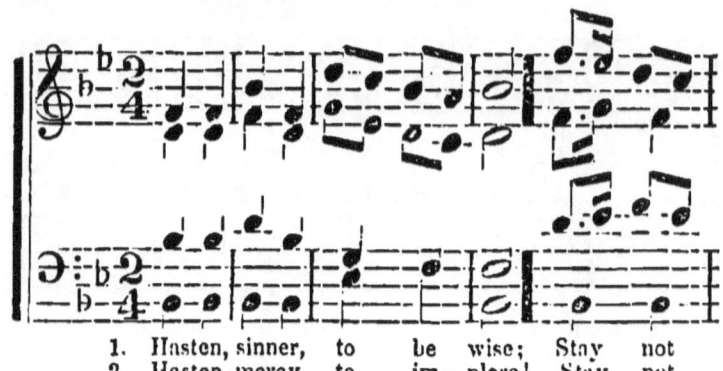

1. Hasten, sinner, to be wise; Stay not
2. Hasten, mercy to im-plore! Stay not
3. Hasten, sinner, to re-turn! Stay not
4. Hasten, sinner, to be blest! Stay not

for the morrow's sun: Wisdom if you still de-
for the morrow's sun: Lest thy season should be
for the morrow's sun: Lest thy lamp should fail to
for the morrow's sun: Lest perdition thee ar-

spise, Hard-er is it to be won.
o'er Ere this evening's stage be run.
burn Ere sal-vation's work be done.
rest Ere the morrow is be gun.

WILMOT. 7s or III. I. C. M. VON WEBER. 191

1. Ho-ly Bi-ble! book di-vine!
2. Mine, to chide me when I rove;
3. Mine, to com-fort in dis-tress
4. Mine, to tell of joys to come,

Precious treasure! thou art mine! Mine to tell me
Mine, to show a Sa-viour's love; Mine, art thou to
If the Ho-ly Spir-it bless; Mine, to show by
And the reb-el sin-ner's doom; O thou precious

whence I came; Mine, to teach me what I am.
guide my feet, Mine, to judge, con-demn, ac-quit.
liv-ing faith Man can tri-umph o-ver death.
book di-vine! Precious treasure! thou art mine.

192 **CHANEY.** 7s & 6s or III. 2. L. MARSHALL.

From the Harpsichord, (published in Boston,) by permission.

1. O - pen, Lord, thy in - ward ear, And
2. From the world of sin, and noise, And

bid my heart re - joice; Bid my qui - et
hur - ry, I with - draw; For the small and

spir - it hear Thy com - fort - a - ble voice,
in - ward voice I wait with hum - ble awe;

193

Nev - er in the whirlwind found, Nor where earth-quakes
Si - lent am I now and still, Dare not in thy

rock the place; Still and si - lent is the sound—
presence move To my wait - ing soul, re - veal

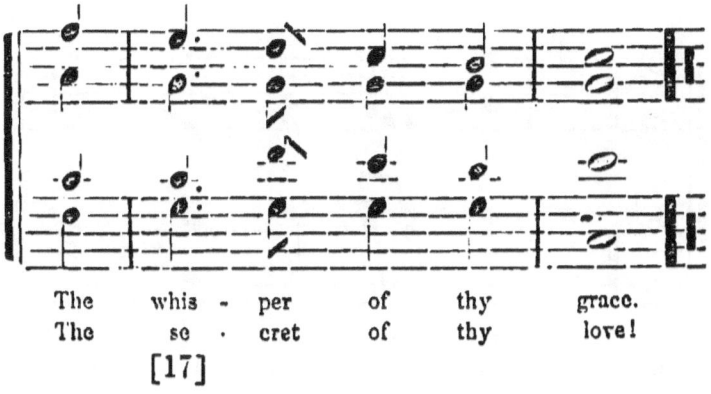

The whis - per of thy grace.
The se - cret of thy love!

[17]

SABBATH. 6s, 8 lines.

Arranged from S. B. POND.

1. The light of Sabbath eve Is
2. To waste these Sabbath hours, O

fading fast a-way; What rec-ord will it
may we nev-er dare; Nor taint with thoughts of

leave To crown the clos-ing day?
ours Those sa-cred days of prayer:

196 HYMN. "The Lord himself." C. M. Double.

M. VERTUE.

1. The Lord himself, the migh - ty Lord, Vouch-

safes to be my guide; The shepherd by whose

con - stant care, My wants are all sup - plied;

2. In ten - der grass he makes me feed, And

gen - tly there re - pose, Then leads me to cool

shades, and where Re - fresh - ing wa - ter flows.
[17*]

198 ACTON. 7s, III. 1. Arranged from WEBER.

1. Je - sus, Lord, we look to thee, Let us
2. By thy rec-on - cil - ing love, Every
3. Free from an-ger and from pride, Let us
4. Let us then with joy re - move To the

in thy name a - gree; Show thy - self the
stumbling - block re - move; Each to each u -
thus in God a - bide; All the depths of
fam - i - ly a - bove; On the wings of

Prince of peace; Bid our jars for - ev - er cease.
- nite, en - dear; Come, and spread thy banner here.
love ex - press, All the heights of ho - li - ness.
an - gels fly; Show how true be - liev-ers die.

ORFORD. 8s, 7s & 4s, or III. 5.

From the "Northern Harp."   Arranged from MADAN.

1. { Men of God! go take your stations; Darkness
   { Loud proclaim a-mong the nations Joy-ful
2. { Go to men in darkness sleeping; Tell that
   { Go to men in bondage weep-ing; Publish

reigns o'er all the earth; }
news of heavenly birth; } Bear the tidings, Tidings of the Saviour's
Christ is strong to save; }
freedom to the slave: } Tell the dying, Christ has triumphed o'er
[the

worth; Bear the ti-dings, Tidings of the Saviour's worth.
grave; Tell the dy-ing, Christ has triumphed o'er the grave.

200 SABBATH SCHOOL HYMN. 8s, 7s, or III. 3.

L. MARSHALL.

From the "Harpsichord," (published in Boston,) by permission.

1. Fa - ther! now the day is passing, Fades the
2. God! I thank thee for the morning; How its
3. Swift - ly sped a - way the morning, Melting
4. Now around us wea - ry children, Night's dark
5. So doth flit life's sun - ny morning, So doth
6. From death's chill and heavy slumbers, God will

glowing light away; Eve - ning gray o'er earth is
freshness filled my frame: Na - ture all hath felt the
in - to yellow noon; Hours of thought and earnest
cur - tain God unfolds; He, who marks the fall - ing
fade life's glowing noon; Life and la - bor must give
call us in - to light; To a morn that knows no

fall - ing, Fit - ting hour for me to pray.
bless - ing, All with me doth praise thy name.
pur - pose, Yet, for ac - tion, fled too soon.
spar - row, Eve - ry sleep - ing frame up - holds.
o - ver, To the shad - ows of the tomb.
fad - ing, To a noon for ev - er bright.

PILGRIM. 7s or 11l. l.   L. MARSHALL.   201

From the "Harpsichord," (published in Boston,) by permission.

1. Come, said Jesus' sacred voice, Come, and
2. Hither come, for here is found, Balm for

make my paths your choice; I will guide you to your
every bleeding wound; Peace which ever shall en-

home, Weary pilgrim, hither come.
dure; Rest eternal, sacred, sure.

BRIGHTNESS. C. P. M. or II. I.

L. MARSHALL.

From the "Harpsichord," (published in Boston,) by permission.

1. My God thy boundless love we praise;
2. 'Tis but love that paints th' purple morn,
3. But in the gos-pel it ap-pears,
4. Then let the love that makes me blest,

How bright on high its glo-ries blaze,
And bids the clouds in air up-borne,
In sweet-er, fair-er char-ac-ters,
With cheer-ful praise in-spire my breast,

How sweet-ly bloom be-low;
Their gen-ial drops dis-til;
And charms the rav-ished breast;
And ar-dent grat-i-tude;

204 HAYDN. 8s, 7s & 4s, or 8s & 7s. HAYDN

1. Sin - ners will you scorn the mes - sage,
2. O, ye an - gels, hov - ering round us,

Sent in mer - cy from a - bove?
Wait - ing spir - its speed your way;

Eve-ry sen - tence, O how ten - der;
Has-ten to the court of heav - en,

BETAH. 7s, or 8s & 7s, or III. I.

C. M. VON WEBER.

1. Softly now the light of day, Fades up-
2. Soon for me the light of day, Shall for-

on my sight a - way; Free from care, from
- ev - er pass a - way; Then, from sin and

la - bor free, Lord I would commune with thee!
sorrow free, Take me, Lord, to dwell with thee!

SENTENCE "The Lord is in his holy temple." 207

L. MARSHALL.

From the "Harpsichord," (published in Boston,) by permission.

SENTENCE. Continued.

SENTENCE. Concluded.

GLORIA PATRI. No. 1. *   MOZART.

211

* In the last part of this piece, the middle notes are for the organ, the highest are for the soprano, and the lower ones on the treble staff are for the alto.

212 GLORIA PATRI. No. 2. CHAPPLE.

213

214 HYMN. "The Last Beam is Shining."

AMERICA. 6s & 4s. 217
WORDS BY S. F. SMITH.

1. My Country! 'tis of thee, Sweet land of lib-er-ty!
2. My na-tive country! thee, Land of the no-ble free!
3. Our Fathers' God, to thee, Author of lib-er-ty!

Of thee I sing;   Land where my fa-thers died; Land of the
Thy name I love; I love thy rocks and rills, Thy woods and
To thee we sing: Long may our land be bright, With freedom's

pilgrim's pride; From ev'ry mountain side, Let freedom ring.
templed hills; My heart with rapture thrills, Like that a-bove.
ho-ly light: Protect us with thy might, Great God our King.

[19]

218 STOCKTON. 7s or III. I. J. H. HEWITT.

Ho - ly Ghost with light di - vine,

Shine upon this heart of mine; Chase the shades of

night a way, Turn the darkness in - to day.

WASHBURN. P. M.   J. H. DANIELS.   219

1. Breast the wave, Christian, When it is strongest, Watch for day,
2. Fight the fight, Christian, Jesus is o'er thee, Run the race
3. Lift the eye, Christian, Just as it closeth, Raise the heart,

Christian, When the night's longest, Onward, and onward still, Be
Christian, Heav'n is before thee; He who hath promised, Faltereth
Christian, Ere it reposeth; Then from the love of Christ, Nothing shall
[thine en-

deavour, The rest that remaineth, Will be for - ev - er.
nev - er, The love of E - ternity, Flows on for - ev - er.
sever, Mount when thy work is done, Praise him forev - er.

220 THE CHRISTIAN PILGRIM 7s, Double.

J. GREGG, Jr. Alexandria, Va.

1. Pil - grim journeying fee - bly on, Smit - ten
2. Let thy spir - it not re - pine, Shade and
3. Christian toil - ing for the prize, Kept for
4. Trembling, hop - ing, filled with pain, Yet re -

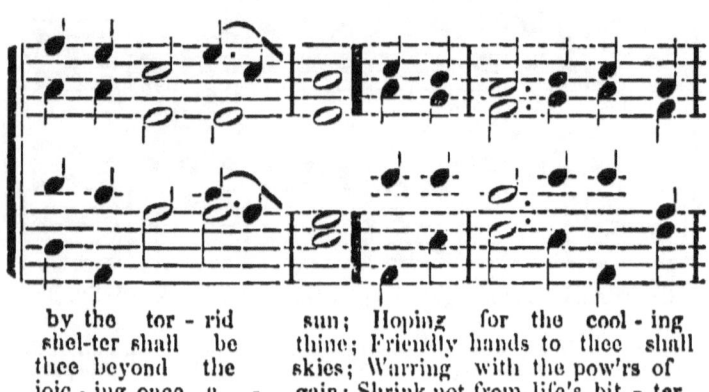

by the tor - rid sun; Hoping for the cool - ing
shel - ter shall be thine; Friendly hands to thee shall
thee beyond the skies; Warring with the pow'rs of
joic - ing once a - gain; Shrink not from life's bit - ter

rain, Look - ing for the shade in vain;
bring, Wa - ter from the cool - ing spring;
sin, Foes with - out and foes with - in;
cup, God shall bear thy spir - it up;

Trav-el-worn and faint at heart, Weak and
And the voice thou lov-est best, Call the
Breathing now in rap-ture's air, Verg-ing
He shall lead thee safe-ly on, 'Till the

wea-ry as thou art, God hath said to com-fort
wand'rer to his rest; God hath said to com-fort
then up-on de-spair, God hath said to com-fort
ark of rest is won, 'Till thy spir-it is set

thee, "As thy days thy strength shall be."
thee, "As thy days thy strength shall be."
thee, "As thy days thy strength shall be."
free, "As thy days thy strength shall be."

[19*]

222 "How lovely is Zion." GEO. F. ROOT.
By permission.

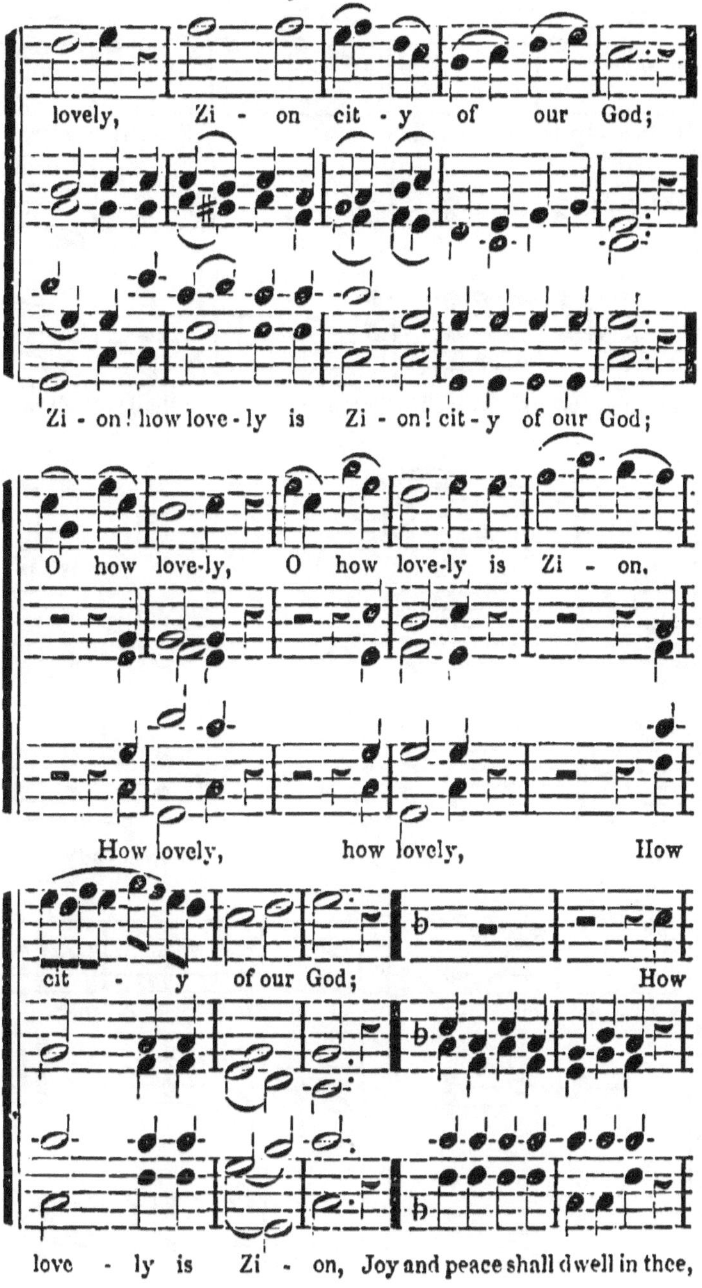
lovely, Zi - on cit - y of our God;
Zi - on! how love - ly is Zi - on! cit - y of our God;
O how love-ly, O how love-ly is Zi - on.
How lovely, how lovely, How
cit - y of our God; How
love - ly is Zi - on, Joy and peace shall dwell in thee,

226 "The Lord will comfort Zion." Continued.

"The Lord will comfort Zion." Concluded. 227

228 GIBBONS. 12s & 11s.

From Root & Sweetzer's Coll. By permission.

1. Thou art gone to the grave— but we
2. Thou art gone to the grave— we no
3. Thou art gone to the grave— and its
4. Thou art gone to the grave— but we

will not de - plore thee, Though sor - rows and
long er be - hold thee, Nor tread the rough
man sion for - sak - ing, Per - chance thy weak
will not de - plore thee, Since God was thy

dark ness en - com - pass the tomb;
paths of the world by thy side;
spir - it in doubt ling - er ed on;
ran - som, thy guard - ian, thy guide;

230 "Come unto me." J. GREGG, JR.

Come un-to me all ye that la - bor,

all ye that la - bor, and are heavy la - den, and

I will give you rest, And I............ will

give you rest; Take my yoke, my yoke up-on you and

learn of me, For I am meek and low-ly of

And ye shall find rest un-
heart, And ye shall find rest........................ un-

WELTON. L. M. 233

Arranged from Rev. C. Malan.

1. Think of her toil, her anxious care, Who form'd thy
2. Nor keep from memory's glad re-view, The fears which
3. When pressed by sickness, pain or grief, How anxious
4. God of our life, each pa-rent guard, And death's sad

lisp - ing lips to prayer, To win for God the
all the fa - ther knew, The joy that marked his
to af - ford re - lief, Our dearest wish they
hour, O long re - tard; Be theirs each joy that

yielding soul, And all its ar - dent thoughts con - trol.
thankful gaze, As virtue crowned ma - tur - er days.
held their own; Till ours returned, their peace was flown.
gilds the past, And Leav'n our mutual home at last.

[20*]

No. 1. SINGLE CHANT.

Arranged from a GREGORIAN.

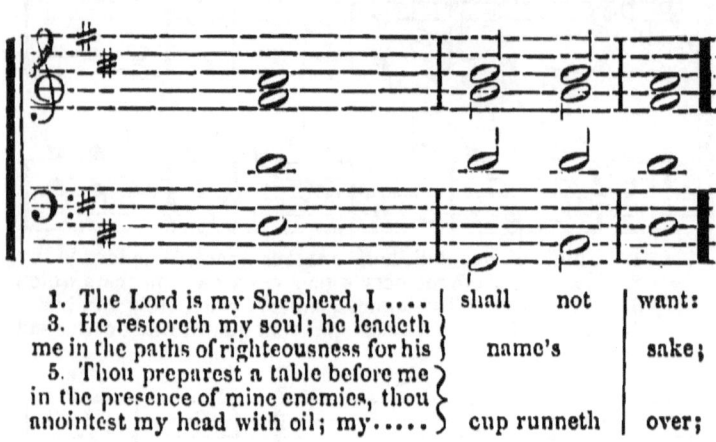

1. The Lord is my Shepherd, I .... | shall not | want:
3. He restoreth my soul; he leadeth me in the paths of righteousness for his | name's | sake;
5. Thou preparest a table before me in the presence of mine enemies, thou anointest my head with oil; my..... | cup runneth | over;

2. He maketh me to lie down in green pastures; he leadeth me be | side the | still | waters.
4. Yea, tho' I walk thro' the valley of the shadow of death, I will fear no evil; for thou art with me; thy rod and thy.... | staff they | comfort | me.
6. Surely goodness and mercy shall follow me all the days of my life; and I will dwell in the house of the | Lord for- | ev - - | - er. A - men.

THE BEATITUDES. Matt. v. 3—12. 235

No. 2. IRREGULAR.

1. Blessed are the poor in spirit: for theirs is the kingdom of |
[heaven.

2. Blessed are they that mourn: for they shall be | comforted.

3. Blessed are the meek: for they shall inherit the | earth.

4. { Blessed are they who do hunger and thirst after righteousness;
   { For they shall be | filled.

5. Blessed are the merciful: for they shall obtain | mercy.

6. Blessed are the pure in heart: for they shall see | God.

7. { Blessed are the peace-makers:
   { For they shall be called the children of | God.

8. { Blessed are they who are persecuted for righteousness sake:
   { For theirs is the kingdom of | heaven.

9. { Blessed are ye, when men shall revile you, and persecute you,
   { And shall say all manner of evil against you falsely for my sake.

10. { Rejoice, and be exceeding glad, for great is your reward in
    [heaven;
    { For so persecuted they the prophets which were be | fore you.

(Hallelujah.)

SINGLE CHANT.

No. 3.

1. Holy, holy, holy, Lord, God Al - | mighty,
   Which was, and | is, and | is to | come.

2. Thou art worthy, O Lord, to receive glory, and | honor, and |
   { For thou hast created all things,   [power;
   { And for thy pleasure they | are and | were cre - | ated.

3. Worthy is the Lamb | that was | slain,
   { To receive power, and riches, and wisdom,
   { And strength; and | honor, and | glory, and | blessing.

4 Blessing, and honor, and | glory and | power,
   { Be unto him that sitteth upon the throne,
   { And unto the | Lamb for - | ever and | ever. **Amen.**

No. 4. **SINGLE CHANT.** 237

Arranged from DE MONTL

1. How amiable are thy tabernacles, O | Lord of | hosts!
2. { My soul longeth, yea, even fainteth for the courts of the Lord;
   { My heart and my flesh crieth | out for the | living | God.

3. { Blessed are they that dwell in thy house;
   { They | will be still | praising thee;
4. { Blessed is the man whose strength is in thee;
   { In whose | heart are the | ways of | them.

5. { They go from strength to strength;
   { Every one of them in Zion ap - | peareth before | God;

6. { O Lord God of hosts, hear my prayer;
   { Give | ear, O | God of | Jacob. (Hallelujah, No. 1.)

7. Behold, O God, our shield, and look upon the face of ' thine
   [an- | ointed.

   { For a day in thy courts is better than a thousand;
8 { I had rather be a door-keeper in the house of my God,
   { Than to | dwell in the | tents of | wickedness.

   { For the Lord God is a sun and a shield; the Lord will give grace
9. {   [and glory:
   { No good thing will he withhold from them that | walk up- |
                                                          [rightly.
10. { O Lord of hosts
    { Blessed is the | man that | trusteth in | thee. (Hallelujah, 2.)

238 No. 5. **SINGLE CHANT.**

1. { Lord, thou hast been our dwelling place
   In | all gene - | rations,

2. { Before the mountains were brought forth.
   Or ever thou hadst formed the earth and the world.
   Even from everlasting to ever | lasting, | Thou art **God.**

3. { Thou turnest man to destruction;
   And sayest, Return, ye | chil-dren of | men.

4. { For a thousand years in thy sight
   Are but as yesterday when it is past,
   And | as a | watch in the | night.

5. { Thou carriest them away as with a flood,
   They are as a sleep,
   In the morning they are like grass which | groweth | up.

6. { In the morning it flourisheth, and groweth up;
   In the evening it is cut | down, *cut* | *down*, and | withereth.

7. { Who knoweth the power of thine anger?
   Even according to thy fear; | so is thy | wrath.

8. { So teach us to number our days,
   That we may ap - | ply our | hear's unto | wisdom.

www.ingramcontent.com/pod-product-compliance
Lightning Source LLC
Chambersburg PA
CBHW031739230426
43669CB00007B/403